The Athletic

Built for This

The Milwaukee Bucks' Historic Run to the 2021 NBA Title

This book is available in quantity at special discounts for your group or organization.

For further information, contact:

Triumph Books LLC
814 North Franklin Street
Chicago, Illinois 60610
Phone: (312) 337-0747
www.triumphbooks.com

Printed in U.S.A.
ISBN: 978-1-62937-960-9

The Athletic
Chris Sprow, Editorial Director
Evan Parker, SVP/GM Content Operations
Sergio Gonzalez, Senior Managing Editor – NBA
Tyler Batiste, Managing Editor – NBA
Rob Peterson, Senior Editor – NBA
Stu Ohler, Design Director
Trevor Gibbons, Partnerships Director
Jenna Winchell, Marketing Director
Amanda Ephrom, Brand Strategist
Olivia Witherite, Social Engagement
Ankur Chawla, Business Operations
Brooks Varni, Editorial Operations

Featured writers from The Athletic
David Aldridge, Sam Amick, Shams Charania, Erik Nehm and Joe Vardon

Special thanks to the entire The Athletic NBA Staff

Content packaged by Mojo Media, Inc.
Joe Funk: Editor
Jason Hinman: Creative Director

Front cover photo by USA Today Sports
Back cover photo by AP Images
Unless otherwise noted, all interior photos by AP Images

Contents

Introduction

By Rob Peterson

If you have picked up this publication to read about the Milwaukee Bucks, you need to know that this introduction has been building for a long time.

Bucks fans were hoping something like it would have been written in 2019, when the Bucks went 10-1 in their first 11 playoff games, complete with a 2-0 lead in the Eastern Conference finals. But ... well, the less said about the ending the better.

Bucks fans were also hoping this intro would have been written in 2020, when the Bucks had the NBA's best record before the COVID-19 pandemic hit. When the season resumed in the NBA bubble, playoff success — for a variety of reasons — again eluded Milwaukee.

But, finally — finally! — in 2021, the pieces came together for the Milwaukee Bucks, as they are the NBA champions, a mere 50 years after the last one.

This championship, however, hasn't been half a century in the making. It's more like 50 years in the waiting.

They were built for this ...

Yet, if one feels compelled to mark a date as to where the Bucks' road to the second title in franchise history began, start on June 27, 2013. That's when the franchise found its championship cornerstone when then-NBA commissioner David Stern announced, "with the 15th pick in the two-thousand and thirteen NBA Draft, the Milwaukee Bucks select..." pausing to make sure he had the correct pronunciation, "Giannis Adet-o-kunbo, from Athens, Greece." The then-18-year-old was long (6-foot-9), and just as long on potential. He was thin (196 pounds), and just as thin on experience. Only hardcore draft geeks knew Giannis Antetokounmpo.

Now, eight years into his career, everyone knows who "The Greek Freak," 2021 Finals MVP, is.

They were built for this ...

You could also point to July 31, 2013, when the other franchise cornerstone, Khris Middleton, was included as a throw-in to the Brandon Jennings-Brandon Knight deal. There have been detractors who have criticized him for not being an adequate complement to Antetokounmpo, but over the course of these past three postseasons, the 6-8 wing has not only been "Khash," he's also been clutch. Middleton averaged 23.6 points per game and hit more shots to tie or give his team the lead in these playoffs than anyone in NBA history.

They were built for this ...

Then, brick by brick, there have been key additions along the way. On Nov. 23, 2020, the Bucks acquired Jrue Holiday in a franchise-altering trade. Some questioned whether the multiple first-round draft picks and swaps were worth it. Throughout the postseason, the defensive stalwart hounded opponents for 94 feet, especially Suns guards Chris Paul and Devin Booker in the Finals, for six games. Was it worth it? Picks for a championship? I would say so.

Three years ago, there were moves for Brook Lopez, Pat Connaughton, and the selection of Donte DiVincenzo in the draft. This season, they brought in Bryn Forbes and Milwaukee folk hero Bobby Portis. There was a mid-year trade for lead "dog" defender and locker room leader P.J. Tucker. All were crucial to the championship run, a journey that was not only about winning, but also exorcising the demons of playoffs past.

In the first round, they swept the Miami Heat, the team that unceremoniously burst the Bucks' bubble in 2020. Middleton hit the Game 1 winner in an overtime thriller and the Bucks never looked back. In the conference semis, they faced their toughest test in the Brooklyn Nets. Down two games, then 3-2, the Bucks proved their championship mettle by winning Game 6 at home and Game 7, in overtime on the road, one of the greatest wins in franchise history. After dispatching a game Atlanta Hawks squad in six games, the Bucks did the same against the Suns.

They were built for this ...

Unlike Bucks teams that have fallen short in the past, this team showed the resilience and the determination that defines what it means to be a champion. There were the 0-2 deficits to the Nets and the Suns, Kevin Durant's nuclear-powered Game 5, the skin-of-their-teeth win in Game 7 and the Game 1 loss to Atlanta. In Game 4 against the Hawks, Antetokounmpo's knee bent as no human knee should. Most everyone, including Antetokounmpo, thought he was done for the year. He missed two games before returning in time for Game 1 of the NBA Finals, where he averaged 35.2 points, 13.2 rebounds and 5 assists and delivered one huge series-changing block in an MVP performance.

So, as you hold this publication in your hand, you're thrilled — and possibly are still processing — that your Bucks are world champions. Will Bucks fans need to wait 'til 2071 before reading another introduction about an NBA title?

If this postseason run is any indication, no it won't take another 50 years, because this team, *they were built for this.* ▬▬

NBA Finals
4-2 Over the Phoenix Suns

Game 1: Suns 118, Bucks 105

Game 2: Suns 118, Bucks 108

Game 3: Bucks 120, Suns 100

Game 4: Bucks 109, Suns 103

Game 5: Bucks 123, Suns 119

Game 6: Bucks 105, Suns 98

Back from the Brink

Supposedly Lost to Injury, Giannis Antetokounmpo Has Found Dominance and Given Bucks a Chance in NBA Finals

By David Aldridge | July 12, 2021

We take things for granted in our instapundit, there-will-be-another-13-year-old-TikTok-star-next-week world these days.

In the matter of what Giannis Antetokounmpo is doing so far in these Finals, that would be a mistake.

It hasn't been two weeks since most of the NBA, including Antetokounmpo, feared he might have blown out his ACL in the Eastern Conference finals against the Hawks and be out a year. Maybe longer.

He was back in a week, with what was diagnosed as a hyperextended knee. And he's still not 100 percent physically. But whatever the number, he's put Andre the Giant-like paws on this series. The Bucks are still down 2-1 after their 120-100 Game 3 rout of Phoenix on Sunday, with Giannis going for 41 points, 13 rebounds and six assists in 38 minutes. But they have a chance because the two-time MVP's first three Finals games — ever — are on a par with what the best who ever played in championship series have achieved.

Apples-to-apples comparisons with the all-timers are impossible. As noted, Antetokounmpo's body of Finals work pales in comparison to that of LeBron James (55 career Finals games), Michael Jordan (35) and others. But Giannis is off to a great start, averaging 34.3 points, 14 rebounds and 4.7 assists in the first three games against the Suns. He's only the second player in Finals history, after Shaquille O'Neal, to post consecutive games with 40 or more points and 10 or more rebounds.

And he's gotten to the free-throw line an astounding 47 times in three games. That he made 13 of 17 from the line in Game 3 was a bonus for the Bucks, but he could go 6 of 17 from the line and it would still have a massive impact on a game.

Giannis Antetokounmpo scored 41 points in Milwaukee's dominant win over Phoenix in Game 3 of the NBA Finals.

"I'm not Michael Jordan," Antetokounmpo almost whispered into the lectern mic after being told that Jordan had scored 40 points in four straight games against the Suns in the '93 Finals.

No, he's not. But he's been pretty damn special.

"He's been the most inspiring player during these playoffs, while (Chris) Paul has been the sentimental player we all root for and want his career to end with a ring," Hall of Famer Isiah Thomas texted Sunday night.

I especially wanted Thomas' perspective because he put on one of the most courageous and incredible performances while similarly injured on the biggest stage — 25 points in the third quarter of Game 6 of the 1988 Finals against the Lakers after severely spraining his ankle early in the quarter. He finished with 43 points in that game, a narrow Pistons loss.

Rare is a two-time league MVP who so often is reminded of what he can't do. It's wild. The guy guts opposing defenses, sets up teammates for wide-open shots game after game, year after year, chases down ridiculous blocks and has lifted a city that has been a basketball afterthought for two decades. There were 25,000 people outside Fiserv Forum, the latest crazed watch party to celebrate the Bucks' ascension to the NBA's elite. (Is it here that I shouldn't say the words "super-spreader event"?) That's all happening here because of one man.

Not the Bronze Fonz.

"Giannis' leadership on and off the court has been legendary!" Thomas said in the text. "Remember it was he and the Milwaukee Bucks that stopped the sports world. His failures at the foul line, his lack of shooting touch from the perimeter and on and on. Yet and still he 'perseveres' with a determination that's rarely seen in sports nowadays. His Brooklyn series will be viewed as one of the all-time best when time moves us further away from the present. He has overcome the failures of his physical body and tapped into basketball's spiritual energy, he doesn't run anymore — he glides with his strides and dominates with his energy and force. Mental is to physical as 4 is to 1. Size and jumping ability can't compete with the physics of energy and force!"

Antetokounmpo had to trust his teammates to get the Bucks past the Hawks in the last two games of the conference finals while he was out. Once he knew his knee was structurally sound and he could play in the Finals, he has returned with an avenging spirit. He abused Jae Crowder and Mikal Bridges and anyone else Phoenix tried to put on him, fighting for loose balls in the paint for and-1s, starting the ball pinwheeling around when the Suns doubled him.

When the Suns didn't double, "now he's just really playing one-on-one," Bobby Portis said. "Good luck with that. For real, for real."

Said Antetokounmpo: "I'm happy that I'm able to be out there, win or lose. It doesn't matter, the outcome. I feel like everybody worked so hard to be in this moment. Me personally, I'm not trying to make it about me. I was happy that I had a chance to come back, and enjoy, play with my teammates, no matter what the outcome is. Just be out there with them."

I asked Thomas where one goes in a time like that — when you are exhausted, mentally and physically, and you see all that you've worked a lifetime for slipping away, because your body — of

After missing the final two games of the Eastern Conference Finals, Giannis Antetokounmpo returned to lead the Bucks against the Suns.

all things! — got injured at the worst possible time.

"I don't have the answer to that question," Thomas said. "It's like in the Baptist Church you get the Holy Ghost and Spirits take over. We know it when we see it and feel it. How you get there is still a mystery."

The sheer audacity of Antetokounmpo becoming the Greek Freak is something about which they'll write books. (Wait a minute ... someone already has!) You can't tell his story enough. It only grows in the retelling. He wasn't just a young boy from an immigrant family trying to make it in a tough section of Athens less than a decade ago; he was part of a community that was looked down upon, rejected. Not worthy. And yet there was something in that Nigerian kid who was born in Greece that wasn't just built to survive; it was shape-shifting. Not just greatness on a basketball court, but being willing to stay and be loyal to the team that drafted him.

I went back this weekend and looked at my pre-draft notes from 2013 when the Bucks wound up taking Antetokounmpo No. 15 overall. He wasn't a secret. A lot of NBA teams had gone over to watch him play with Filathlitikos, a team in the Greek B Basket League, not the top Greek Basket (A1) League that features traditional powers Olympiacos and Panathinaikos. Scouts saw something in him, but they didn't seem to know what. And they certainly didn't see this.

"A little bit of a hype behind it," one team executive said at the time. "A slower 6-7. Not (Nicolas) Batum, my friend. A lot of conflicting reports, but the guys who've seen him have told me not to get too excited."

Said another: "Long-term project, very young, still raw. If you're willing to wait the three years, probably, maybe four years. That alone makes it hard to gauge because he isn't playing against the top teams. But his body is impressive. His brother's good, but I didn't get the sense that the brother was quite the prospect, but that he was good. I can't imagine how he plays in the league for a couple of years, maybe longer. Especially the way the rules are. You have to absorb the cap hit over the summer so you really lessen your ability to spend money."

Said a third: "He is intriguing. He's 6-9, and all of it long. The problem with those guys is when do you pick them and what's the body of work? For me, we've been noticing ... I try to follow these guys from a certain age. There has to be a body of work. ... This guy is young, but it's a risk. There's a chance, but he doesn't have the body of work ... it's the same sexiness that's lured us into some players who haven't worked. He's shown some skills. When he played for the junior team, he played some point guard, but it's the same Batum had, the same (Evan) Fournier had. You can be intrigued by them as point guards, but you don't know what their position is going to be."

Said a fourth: "In my opinion, he needs to stay. Very long, thin body. Big ol' hands. He needs to come in a year later. He played in a low division He's not ready yet. Very, very skilled, very talented. Somebody's gonna pick him. If he does stay in, I would say second round. But I think he should go back."

Now, they weren't wrong in that, at the time — Antetokounmpo was rail-thin and was just starting to fill out. But most of them were wrong — loud wrong. Only one guy seemed to see something in Giannis that the others didn't.

"I walked out of there saying holy cow, this kid's a freak," the executive said in 2013. "He has no body. He's got pipe fitter legs. But he's got Magic Johnson kind of handle and court vision. ... what I saw was a guy who can handle it, who can make plays. People are going to want to make him a point guard. He might be a point forward at the end of the day ... he would be a project. It's not like with many African kids where you're teaching

P.J. Tucker extends to reach for the ball during the first half of Game 3. Tucker contributed seven points, three rebounds and two steals in the Bucks' victory.

them how to play basketball. This kid knows how to play basketball ... he doesn't have crazy, crazy hops to go with that length, but the combination of his athleticism and his length is pretty scary."

(I would tell you who it was but, I don't know, guys tell me this stuff in confidence. Even when they turn out to be right, they still told you in confidence, you know? Maybe I'll give his name some day.)

Antetokounmpo's son Liam, now 15 months old, was crawling around the interview room while his father spoke after Game 3. When he was done, he scooped little Liam up and carried him into the July night. Liam is not yet old enough to understand the fresh, historical earth his dad is plowing, ignoring the pain and the limitations and the fear that were front of mind just a fortnight ago, willing his team to places it hasn't been in a generation — but which now can dream of reaching again and again, with his audaciousness and talents in full flower, for all the world to see. ▬▬▬

From 'Oh, S—t!' to 'Shock'

How Giannis Antetokounmpo's Iconic Block Saved the Bucks' Season

By Sam Amick and Eric Nehm | July 15, 2021

So here's the thing about LeBron James' epic Finals block, the one in 2016 that became part of the NBA conversation again late Wednesday night when Giannis Antetokounmpo did something so majestic, so monumental, that an instant debate ensued about where it ranked in the history of such feats.

J.R. Smith never gets any credit. Yes, LeBron flew like he had his own airline after chasing down Andre Iguodala in a Game 7 moment that is widely considered the best block in Finals lore. But it was Smith, the Cleveland guard who had been chasing the Golden State swingman step for step down the floor, who bought time for James' swat against the backboard that all but saved the Cavaliers' first and only title. Truth be told, it was a two-man effort.

But when Phoenix Suns big man Deandre Ayton took off from the left side of the paint for what appeared to be a sure alley-oop dunk late in the fourth quarter of Game 4 against Milwaukee, there was only one man who had any chance of stopping the play that came with the Bucks up 101-99 and 1:15 to go. It was Antetokounmpo, the 26-year-old who the great Shaquille O'Neal once dubbed "the new Superman."

And without his block, that remarkable display of instincts, IQ and athleticism in which he read the lob pass that was coming from Devin Booker and recovered in time to take flight and swat Ayton's shot away while keeping the Suns at bay, the Bucks would likely find themselves in the kind of 3-1 hole that only James' Cavs have been able to survive. Instead, after Khris Middleton scored Milwaukee's next seven points on his 40-point outing and the Bucks held on for the 109-103 win to tie the series 2-2, their hopes for the franchise's first title since 1971 are alive again heading into Game 5 in Phoenix on Saturday.

But first, behold this deeper appreciation of the memorable play that saved the Bucks' season and sparked such rigorous debate afterward about how it should be

Giannis Antetokounmpo blocks Deandre Ayton's alley-oop dunk attempt late in the fourth quarter of Game 4.

remembered. And for what it's worth, all of the above perspective was written before Bucks guard Pat Connaughton — as you'll see below — went to great lengths to rank the Antetokounmpo block above the iconic James play that came with an assist of sorts from Smith.

The following is perspective on the play from the Bucks who had the best view on the floor. Quotes have been lightly edited for brevity and clarity.

Antetokounmpo, who finished with 26 points, 14 rebounds, eight assists and two blocks and is now the clear leader for Finals MVP honors (he's averaging 32.3 points on 61.3 percent shooting, 14 rebounds, 5.5 assists, 1.8 steals and 1.5 blocks per game in the series).

Just a hustle play. I thought I was going to get dunked on, to be honest with you. But you know, going down the stretch, just do whatever it takes to win the game. Just put yourself in a position that can win the game. I saw the play coming. I saw that (Booker) was going to throw the lob and I was just going to jump vertical toward the rim. Hopefully I can be there in time, and I was there in time and was able to get a good block.

I saw it coming. Once I saw (Booker) put (the ball) in his one hand, he was too far for a layup. So I knew he was trying to lob, and I committed so much. You risk it. You kind of feel it. I felt (Ayton) rolling to the rim behind me, so I knew the only chance to get a stop is just jump toward the rim and try to cover that angle for him to score.

(But) I was late. Usually a play like that, if I was on the opposite side, it's a dunk. But as I said, I didn't jump to block the ball. I jumped toward the rim. I feel like that's what kind of helped me put me in position to get the block. The rim was right here (motions with his hands) so I jumped right here (motions with his hands). So he could shoot the ball. If he shot the ball to the backboard, it's

probably goaltending. He tried to dunk it, and I was right there earlier than him.

Jrue Holiday, the Bucks point guard who struggled offensively (four of 20 shooting) but continues to bother Suns point guard Chris Paul defensively (five of 13 shooting, five turnovers and a minus-10 rating). On the Antetokounmpo block, Holiday was on the right side of the lane, watching helplessly while Booker threw the lob to the left.

That's elite. That's an elite block, to be able to read that he's going to throw the lob and go up there and get it, yeah, that's elite. (I recognized the play) about the same time (as Antetokounmpo), but what can I do about it? Ayton's seven feet. Again, Giannis is athletic, but I just think his IQ for the game and to be able to read that and especially the point in the game that it was in, just makes it a very elite block.

Pat Connaughton, who was guarding the Suns' Jae Crowder on the left wing when Ayton rolled to the rim. Connaughton, who had 11 points, nine rebounds and was a plus-21, could do little more than motion for Antetokounmpo to track down the big man while standing on the perimeter.

Yeah, I was on Crowder. (Antetokounmpo) was pulling up (defensively) after the pick-and-roll. I was thinking I was right around the elbow at the time. And the honest thought that was going through my head was more or less kind of like shock and awe. When the block happened, I kind of looked like — and luckily P.J. (Tucker) came across the lane and grabbed the rebound because I forgot for a split-second to go grab it.

In my opinion, it's the best block of all time. Obviously, we're a little biased and you can talk about the LeBron block as well. But as far as a block where he was covering the pick-and-roll, he had to judge where the pass was, where Ayton was

Giannis Antetokounmpo's blocked shot prevented Phoenix from tying the game with 1:14 remaining in the fourth quarter. Teammate Pat Connaughton called the play "the best block of all time."

catching it and trying to dunk it, above the box, it's about as impressive as you can get.

James' block, for the record, came with the score tied 89-89 and 1:51 remaining in the fourth.

I would look at the criteria of greatest block of all time based off of difficulty of the block and then time and score. I think obviously LeBron's time and score probably has the edge in that situation because of when it was and helped them literally win a championship that game. But I think the difference between the time and score difference and then the difficulty of the block difference, gives the edge to Giannis just because a chase-down block, you have a little bit more of an ability to read, and obviously it's a great block and we're talking about two of the greatest blocks of all time and I don't want to discredit that block.

But Giannis was guarding the pick-and-roll. He was guarding the pick-and-roll. That's a play that they have done time and time again. Book threw a great pass, threw it high and away from any defender and Giannis was able to recover. He's Defensive Player of the Year, two-time MVP for a reason and I think it's those types of plays to be able to read where Ayton is, where the ball is, and to have the athleticism to get that high and get literally all of the basketball is why I would give the edge to him.

Middleton, whose midrange jumper from above the foul line seconds before the block put the Bucks up, on what was going through his mind as the lob pass was thrown (he was on the right side near Holiday).

Excuse my language, but it was one of those 'Oh shit' moments. We gave up a layup (on the prior possession) and next thing you know he's blocking it. It was a great effort. Didn't give up on the play when it seemed like they had (an) open layup or dunk. That's what we need in the Finals.

Everybody (gives) that extra effort and he came through for us big on that play.

Bucks coach Mike Budenholzer.

Giannis just made a spectacular block, spectacular play. His ability to cover ground and get to that point, get to the top. That's an NBA Finals special moment right there, and we're going to need more of them. His impact on the game on both ends of the court — it's a big-time block. That's what he's capable of.

Antetokounmpo, who shared a brief flex with the baseline fans after the block and before running back on offense.

Tough game. Tough game. It wasn't a pretty game, but we grinded through. They played really good, really good. You have to give them credit. But as I said, three minutes before in the timeout in my head, I'm like, 'You've got to keep making plays; right now, it's how bad do you want it?' If they go up 3-1, it's a whole different ballgame.

I feel like it was just emotions (after the block). Sometimes I block shots and I run the other way, but I think there was so much emotions into me and I tried to enjoy that moment. And there's some times that you have a block, you have a three, whatever, run to the other end. But for me, the way I play, the way I want to play moving forward, I want to enjoy every single moment. That was a moment that I felt like our team was turning it around and we were getting momentum and Khris was hitting big shots. It felt good. So yeah, to answer your question, it felt good, and the way we were playing felt good at the time. ▬▬

In addition to his game-saving block, Giannis Antetokounmpo contributed 26 points, 14 rebounds and eight assists in Game 4.

Valley-Oop, the Sequel

How Giannis Antetokounmpo Stayed in the Moment After Missed Free Throws to Dunk the Bucks to the Verge of a Title

By Sam Amick | July 18, 2021

What if Giannis Antetokounmpo had frozen?

What if, after missing those two crucial free throws with 1:09 left in the fourth quarter of Game 5 of the NBA Finals on Saturday night at the Suns' arena, when Phoenix Suns coach Monty Williams tried to mess with his mind by calling that timeout after his first attempt and Jae Crowder and Chris Paul tried to get under his skin before the second, the Milwaukee Bucks star went into the kind of psychological shell that wouldn't have made his latest iconic play possible?

This is everything Antetokounmpo had talked about the day before, when an off-day media session with reporters turned into a clinic on sports psychology — heck, life lessons really — after I'd asked the 26-year-old to explain his refreshing perspective on the topic of ego. The NBA's most reluctant superstar had finally been opening up on this global stage in recent days, sharing all the parts of his psyche that have played a pivotal part in his rise, and we were all starting to truly understand the unique and admirable way in which he's wired.

"I figured out a mindset to have that when you focus on the past, that's your ego," he had said. "I did this. We were able to beat this team 4-0. I did this in the past. I won that in the past. When I focus on the future, it's my pride. Yeah, next game, Game 5, I do this and this and this. I'm going to dominate. That's your pride talking. It doesn't happen. You're right here.

"I kind of try to focus on the moment, in the present," he added. "That's humility. That's being humble. That's not setting no expectation. That's going out there, enjoying the game, competing at a high level. I think I've had people throw throughout my life that helped me with that. But that is a skill that I've tried to, like, kind of — how do you say, perfect it."

Giannis Antetokounmpo finishes the alley-oop from Jrue Holiday, effectively clinching the pivotal Game 5 win and immediately going down as one of the most memorable plays in NBA Finals history.

So here he was, staying present, staying locked in, enjoying the struggle and competing with the kind of humble spirit that allows him to have a clear mind when it matters most. There were 18,000-plus Suns fans inside the newly named Footprint Center mockingly counting while he shot those free throws and screaming when he failed. Even the slightest bit of brain freeze, or embarrassment, could have cost them this 123-119 win and the chance to take a 3-2 series lead heading into Game 6 in Milwaukee on Tuesday.

But 56 seconds later, after the Suns' Devin Booker drove into the lane with Milwaukee up 120-119 and was trapped by Antetokounmpo, P.J. Tucker and Jrue Holiday, a play unfolded that required his full focus. Holiday's strip sent the ball into the air, and the point guard whose 27-point, 13-assist outing was so welcomed by the Bucks after his offensive struggles in Game 4 was on his way from there.

Four Suns trailed the play, with Booker laying face down on the hardwood and Paul defending all by his lonesome in transition. Cue those long Antetokounmpo strides that never get old to watch — 13 in all once the break began leading into his alley-oop in the clouds from Holiday.

The genius of what Holiday did was in the set-up. Despite being fully capable of taking Paul to the rim, he floated to the left wing and drew the Suns point guard out as a result. Enter Antetokounmpo, who barreled through the lane and launched off of the same left leg that was in question entering this series.

Those fears of an ACL tear might feel like they took place months ago at this point, but it should not be forgotten that it was June 29 when Antetokounmpo's leg bent backward and he went through intense pain. This play wasn't as spectacular as his iconic block in Game 4 — the one that also required ample explosion from that ailing left knee — but it was game-saving for the Bucks and soul-sucking for the Suns nonetheless.

"Giannis took off (down the floor) and he was calling for the ball," Holiday said. "So at that point, I just threw it as high as I could and only where Giannis could go get it, and he went up there got it."

Antetokounmpo took off from just outside of the restricted area, then barely got a grip on the ball for the dunk just as his massive frame was flying toward the baseline. And just as he did on the block of Deandre Ayton three nights before, he stood and stared at the fans while holding his landing pose.

As Antetokounmpo would share in great detail, conventional wisdom would have mandated that the Bucks pulled the ball out in that scenario. There were only 16 seconds left when Holiday crossed halfcourt, so you burn clock and wait for the Suns to foul, right? Except for one thing: Antetokounmpo, who finished with 32 points, nine rebounds and six assists but missed seven of 11 free throws in all, was calling for the ball.

"He trusted me and made an incredible pass, also, for the lob," Antetokounmpo said. "It was big time. It was a big-time play. It was the winning play of the game. I saw him going there. I saw Chris Paul and then I started sprinting, and I saw nobody was around me. He didn't want to throw me the ball at first, but I was like, Throw it, throw it, throw it.

"And then he threw it. He trusted me. After the game I was like, Thank you for trusting me. He could throw it and make a wrong pass and that would be on him as the point guard. The coach would say, You're supposed to keep the ball. But he trusted me and he knows I'm going to finish the play. That says a lot to me. I went up to him after the game and I told him that, too."

From the court to the press room, there's a directness to Antetokounmpo's communication style that seems to work extremely well. Case in point: the media sessions during these Finals in which he has been so forthright about how he plays this game and where it fits within the context of his life.

His recent joke about having to "tinkle" during games was humanizing, as was his revelation about our hotel lobby conversation that only took place because he'd lost his room key. He listens closely to questions, and offers the kind of authentic answers that are always the goal of us scribes in these types of settings.

So when he abruptly exited the media room on Saturday night, having sat down briefly in front of the microphone before mumbling "I can't" and exiting stage left, it was odd, to say the least. It was unclear whether he would be back, and a league official would later reveal that Antetokounmpo refused a chance to simply answer a few questions with a single reporter and have those answers shared with the masses (it's called a pool report, and it's nowhere near as insightful as a conventional press conference). After approximately a half-hour, with the Suns players and coaches having spoken long before and our limited media crew of approximately 15 vaccinated reporters patiently waiting to speak with Antetokounmpo, he finally returned.

"I was a little bit dehydrated," he would later say. "I'm a softy, but it's okay."

To say the least.

Antetokounmpo, the Finals MVP frontrunner who now finds himself one win away from NBA lore, is hard at work trying to get this job done.

"Yeah, it's being in the moment," he said. "You know, not going to lie, I'm always real. I feel like that's what makes me who I am. I'm always real. Sometimes I go to the free throw line and I'm nervous a little bit, you know, but this time, I wasn't nervous at all because I was so dialed in. I just missed.

"But I'm happy. I live with it because I shot my routine, I did exactly what I always do, and I just missed. But there's going to be times that they are going to talk, the opposing players are going to talk, the crowd is going to yell. But just got to keep playing through that. Keep playing, keep your composure and just keep trying to do whatever is possible to help the team win. Like even when we missed (another crucial free throw with 13.5 seconds left, after a Paul foul on the dunk put him to the line again), we were able to tip the ball back to Khris (Middleton) and he made (one of two free throws after getting fouled). I could put my head down and just be like, oh, missed the free throw, whatever the case might be, but no, I kept playing. That's what I do. That's how I'm built." ▬▬

Finally!

Giannis Antetokounmpo's Historic 50-point Game Leads Bucks to First NBA Title in 50 years

By Eric Nehm | July 20, 2021

The Milwaukee Bucks finally did it.

Fifty years after Kareem Abdul-Jabbar and Oscar Robertson led the Bucks to the franchise's first championship in 1971, just the team's third season of existence, the Bucks have won their second NBA title. In doing so, Giannis Antetokounmpo proved all the naysayers wrong and showed that he could bring a championship to the team that drafted him — and the small midwestern city that embraced him — from that moment on June 27, 2013.

And in his first NBA Finals, Antetokounmpo delivered more than anyone could have ever expected.

In Game 6, with the Bucks one win away from securing an NBA title, Antetokounmpo played a game for the ages and put up 50 points, 14 rebounds, two assists and five blocks in 42 minutes. The rest of the Bucks struggled offensively in Game 6, but it didn't matter; Antetokounmpo took over in the second half, scoring 33 points on 10-of-15 shooting while going a scorching 12 of 13 from the free-throw line.

"I don't know how many words you need to use beyond 50 points in a close-out game in an NBA Finals," Bucks center Brook Lopez said. "Pretty much sums it all up. It's so indicative of who Giannis is as a player, as a person. He has that mindset always to just take care of business and he's been our leader throughout my time. To have him as a focal point of everything we do and the way he goes about it, it's just contagious with the whole team, and he's so impressive night-in and night-out.

"I mean, I told you before, this is stuff you don't want to take for granted. But that's Giannis. That's what he does, and it's just, I mean, completely awe-inspiring. His performance tonight, this whole series, this whole year, there's no words for that.

"You've just got to look at the numbers."

With his Game 6 performance, Antetokounmpo became the first player in NBA Finals history to put up at least 40 points, 10 rebounds and five blocks in a single game. He also

After a historic performance, Giannis Antetokounmpo cradles the Larry O'Brien trophy and the Bill Russell Finals MVP trophy. Antetokounmpo sported a shirt honoring longtime Bucks play-by-play announcer Jim Paschke during the post-game celebrations.

joined Shaquille O'Neal as just the second player in NBA history to put together three games with at least 40 points and 10 rebounds in a single NBA Finals. He was the clear and deserving choice for 2021 NBA Finals MVP, averaging 35.2 points, 13.0 rebounds, 5.0 assists and 1.8 blocks over the Finals.

Antetokounmpo was thrilled to have delivered the title to Milwaukee, especially after signing his supermax deal just before this season started.

"But coming back, I was like, 'This is my city. They trust me. They believe in me. They believe in us,'" Antetokoumpo said while cradling the Larry O'Brien trophy and the Bill Russell Finals MVP trophy. "Even when we lost, the city was still — went outside and you know, obviously I wanted to get the job done.

"But that's my stubborn side. It's easy to go somewhere and go win a championship with somebody else. It's easy. I could go — I don't put — I could go to a super team and just do my part and win a championship. But this is the hard way to do it and this is the way to do it and we did it. Fuckin' did it. We did it, man."

Winning a championship in the 2020-21 season, delayed and mutated by the COVID-19 pandemic, was a struggle for the Bucks, but the title serves as a fitting ending to the team's journey that began when then-general manager John Hammond took a chance on a skinny, unknown forward from Greece in the 2013 NBA Draft. The Bucks won just 15 games in Antetokounmpo's first season, but the team's struggles allowed then-head coach Larry Drew to play Antetokounmpo more than most anyone expected before the season and Antetokounmpo did not disappoint.

Despite playing only five minutes, Antetokounmpo managed to score his first NBA points in the first quarter of his first NBA game. He did so at Madison Square Garden, the NBA's grandest regular-season stage, by getting fouled on the fast break, the portion of the game he would weaponize like few before him, on a pass from Khris Middleton, the man who would be his teammate for the next eight seasons, with Mike Breen, who called each of his spectacular 2021 NBA Finals moments, on the telecast.

His first point that came on the second free throw following the foul was a fun bit of foreshadowing to the triumphant end of the journey on Tuesday night, but the path to the championship was grueling.

Despite signing a group of veteran free agents during the offseason expected to once again keep the Bucks in the bottom of the Eastern Conference playoff picture, the Bucks lost 67 games in Antetokounmpo's rookie season and eventually the Bucks' new ownership group, led by Wes Edens and Marc Lasry, decided to bring in a new coach. With the hiring of Jason Kidd as head coach and No. 2 overall pick Jabari Parker in tow, a sense of optimism grew around the team. It even led a 19-year-old Antetokounmpo to send a tweet Bucks fans would cherish (and bookmark) for the next decade: "I'll never leave the team and the city of Milwaukee till we build the team to a championship level team.."

At the time, did Antetokounmpo understand the statement he was making?

"I didn't (understand) it. I wouldn't make that statement. But that's what I believed. I believed," Antetokounmpo said. "You know little kids are very honest? You know, a five-year-old kid, I might be gaining some pounds, and he goes, you're fat, like brutally honest? That was me at that point. I was so honest. After the Summer League, we played four games, five games, and we like lost all of them.

"I was like, OK, I'm going to win a championship with Milwaukee. I'm going to do whatever it takes in order for me to win it. And we did it. We did it, man. This was an amazing journey. The outcome was great, but even if the outcome wasn't great, thank you for doing your job. It was easy to deal with you guys. Khris, take it. Do your thing."

For the next four seasons under Kidd, Bucks fans watched as Antetokounmpo grew from a lanky question mark to one of the game's most dominant forces.

The debate over how much credit Kidd deserves for the transformation will continue as long as Kidd continues forward as an NBA coach, but the results were undeniable. Antetokounmpo became a solid rotation player during his sophomore campaign and then exploded into stardom after the All-Star Break in his third season when Kidd turned him loose as the Bucks' point guard. Antetokounmpo averaged 18.8 points, 8.6 rebounds and 7.2 assists per game in the season's final 28 games and then signed a four-year, $100 million extension to remain in Milwaukee.

Antetokounmpo's time at point guard set the stage for Antetokounmpo's first All-Star appearance and All-NBA nod in the 2016-17 season, his fourth in the NBA. Antetokounmpo led the Bucks in all five major statistical categories — 22.9 points, 8.8 rebounds, 5.4 assists, 1.9 blocks and 1.6 steals per game — that season on his way to 2nd Team All-NBA honors and his first playoff appearance as the Bucks' leading man (second playoff appearance overall). The Bucks' budding superstar further improved those numbers the next season (26.9 points, 10.0 rebounds and 4.8 assists per game) as he picked up his second straight 2nd Team All-NBA nod, but the team did not improve enough overall and Bucks' ownership fired Kidd before the regular season ended.

Despite Antetokounmpo's individual success,

the Bucks hit a wall as a team. They managed to make the postseason in three of Kidd's four seasons, but never won more than 44 games, advanced past the first round nor started a series as the higher seed. For Antetokounmpo and the Bucks to take the next step, they needed a new coach.

Enter Mike Budenholzer.

In his first season in Milwaukee, the Bucks exploded. They won 60 regular season games for the first time since the 1980-81 season behind Antetokounmpo's first MVP season and the first All-Star season for Middleton, who developed quietly in the shadows right alongside Antetokounmpo. In addition to their two tentpole players, Bucks general manager Jon Horst traded for Eric Bledsoe during the previous season and signed Brook Lopez for the bi-annual extension during the offseason. Throw in Malcolm Brogdon, a second-round selection from the 2016 NBA Draft, and the Bucks were the best regular-season team in the NBA.

Their success continued in the postseason as the Bucks swept the Pistons, dispatched the Celtics in just five games and then took the first two games of the Eastern Conference Finals at home against the Raptors. After winning 10 of their first 11 postseason games though, the Bucks hit a wall. More accurately, Antetokounmpo hit the defensive wall built by the Raptors, featuring Kawhi Leonard, Marc Gasol, Kyle Lowry, Pascal Siakiam and Danny Green. The Raptors' defensive talent and togetherness overwhelmed Antetokounmpo, who spent the rest of the season and postseason slithering through defenses and dominating at the rim in the offensive system Budenholzer built specifically for him.

The Bucks dropped four straight games and their season ended just two wins away from the NBA Finals.

"I want to be more skilled," Antetokounmpo

told The Athletic after the Raptors eliminated the Bucks. "I want to make my game easier."

And the Bucks spent their second season under Budenholzer working on improving the model they created in his first season as head coach in Milwaukee. After putting up the league's best defensive season in the 2018-19 season, the Bucks perfected their defense and shaved off three points per 100 possessions to put together a historically good defense that allowed just 101.6 points per 100 possessions, the league's lowest number by a wide margin. Offensively, they tinkered with using their players in slightly different ways to make their attack more dynamic. Middleton shot more mid-range jumpers, Antetokounmpo worked from the block more often, and Lopez returned to the post like he did when he was an All-Star with the Nets instead of a floor-spacing, 3-point-shooting center.

The Bucks were rolling and then COVID-19 shut down the world.

The league shut down for months before the season restarted on the campus of Walt Disney World near Orlando, Fla. The Bucks struggled to regain their form in the final eight games of the season they played in the NBA bubble, dropping five of eight, and then they even lost Game 1 of their first-round series against the No. 8-seeded Magic before winning three straight games to regain control of the series.

Then, the Bucks shut down the NBA bubble by refusing to take the floor for Game 5 against the Magic on Aug. 26 in the wake of the police shooting of Jacob Blake, a 29-year-old Black man in Kenosha. For two days, the NBA halted as the players and owners attempted to figure out how to better address social justice and racial inequality as a league. Eventually the Bucks and Magic got on the floor on Aug. 29, and Milwaukee closed out the series with an easy win to set up a second-round matchup with the Miami Heat.

And just like the previous season, the Bucks were overwhelmed by the Heat's physical defense. Head coach Erik Spoelstra drew up the plan and again Antetokounmpo repeatedly ran into the wall built by the Heat defense as the Bucks failed to find an answer for the second straight postseason and lost to the Heat in just five games. Antetokounmpo left Game 4 after spraining his ankle in the second quarter and did not play in Game 5, but the Bucks were not going to win the series even with a healthy Antetokounmpo.

So the Bucks made some serious changes, and they did so during what was possibly the most important offseason in the franchise's history as the Bucks had until the first game of the 2020-21 season to convince Antetokounmpo to sign a supermax extension that could keep him in Milwaukee through the 2025-26 season.

Horst started the franchise's makeover with the roster. On the first day trades were allowed, Horst swung two massive deals. First, he moved Eric Bledsoe, George Hill, three first-round picks and two future pick swaps to the Pelicans for All-Star point guard Jrue Holiday. Then, just over an hour later, the Bucks and Kings reportedly agreed to the framework of a sign-and-trade deal that would send Donte DiVincenzo, Ersan Ilyasova and D.J. Wilson to Sacramento for Kings wing Bogdan Bogdanovic.

The Bogdanovic deal was eventually rescinded though as the Bucks were charged with tampering and lost a second-round pick for their dealings with the Kings and Horst filled out the roster by signing big man Bobby Portis, point guard D.J. Augustin, and wing Torrey Craig, as well as re-signing Pat Connaughton.

And then the Bucks waited as Antetokounmpo contemplated one of the biggest decisions of his life. And they waited a little longer. And they waited a little longer. And they waited a little longer until Antetokounmpo ultimately decided to sign the supermax extension to stay in Milwaukee on Dec. 15, 2020.

By signing the extension, Antetokounmpo committed to the team that first committed to him all the way back in 2013. He committed to his teammates, whether it was his longest-teammate, Middleton, or the new players that Horst had added to the roster during the offseason. He committed to the city of Milwaukee, the midwestern city that has not seen a championship since 1971 and embraced Antetokounmpo and his family with open arms and made him one of its most beloved citizens. And most of all, he committed to winning a championship.

With the roster in place, Budenholzer went

to work on giving the team a new look on both sides of the ball. When the Bucks players walked into the first day of training camp, they were greeted by new shapes on the floor as Budenholzer decided to work on a new offense that emphasized "the dunker" area underneath the basket and moved the Bucks' ballhandlers to the wings for their drives. Throughout the season, the Bucks struggled defensively as they attempted to integrate different defensive tactics in order to be more flexible for the postseason, a process that took an extra step when Horst made his final major roster move of the season and traded for Rockets forward P.J. Tucker.

With the new roster and tactics, the Bucks sacrificed regular season success and moved into the playoffs as the No. 3 seed in the East for a series against the team that vanquished them from the postseason the previous season, the Heat. After refusing to put Antetokounmpo on Heat star Jimmy Butler last postseason, Budenholzer unleashed a new defensive strategy against the Heat that matched Antetokounmpo up head-to-head with Butler. After a nail-biting finish in Game 1 capped by a game winner by Middleton, the Bucks rolled to a sweep against the Heat in the first round to set up a tilt against the Nets, the favorites in Las Vegas to win the NBA title.

The Bucks went down 2-0 to the Nets with an embarrassing 39-point loss in Game 2 to set up a must-win Game 3 in Milwaukee. The Bucks prevailed in that game behind rugged defense from Tucker on Kevin Durant and used the momentum to take Game 4 as well before losing Game 5 in Brooklyn as Durant tallied 49 points, 17 rebounds and 10 assists in a 114-108 win for the Nets. The Bucks staved off elimination in Game 6 to set up a do-or-die Game 7. Durant scored 48 points and nailed a long two-pointer to force overtime late in the fourth quarter, but the Bucks managed to fight off the potential heartbreak and advance to the Eastern Conference Finals.

Favored against the Hawks, the Bucks dropped Game 1 as Trae Young put up 48 points, seven rebounds and 11 assists in Fiserv Forum. They recovered to take the next two games before disaster hit in Game 4 and Antetokounmpo hyperextended his left knee in the third quarter and the Hawks tied the series heading back to

Milwaukee. With hushed tones in the bowels of State Farm Arena in Atlanta, Holiday, Middleton and Tucker talked to reporters about how they would try to move forward without their star while being forced to contemplate the possibility of Antetokounmpo being unable to return to the floor this postseason.

"We still gonna win," Tucker told reporters after the game. "This is not how this series is going to go because this can't be how ... like I gotta ... That's all that's going through my mind."

And they did. The Bucks responded to the possible heartbreak and took Games 5 and 6 behind spectacular offensive performances by Holiday, Lopez and Middleton to advance to the NBA Finals and set the stage for Antetokounmpo's return.

Despite suffering one of the more gruesome-looking injuries of his career, Antetokounmpo returned to the floor for Game 1 against the Suns. He played well with 20 points and 17 rebounds, but that performance did not at all hint at the explosion coming in Game 2. In Games 2 and 3, Antetokounmpo became just the second player in NBA history to put up at least 40 points and 10 rebounds in consecutive games. His 41 points, 13 rebounds and six assists in Game 3 led the Bucks to their first NBA Finals victory since 1974, his unbelievable block in the final few minutes of Game 4 helped the Bucks send the series back to Phoenix tied at 2-2, and his alley-oop dunk following Jrue Holiday's steal sealed the Bucks' Game 5 win with an exclamation.

All of which set the stage for Game 6 in Fiserv Forum, the building which the new ownership group built with a parting $100 million gift from Sen. Herb Kohl to keep the team in Milwaukee, the only American city Antetokounmpo has called home. And to no one's surprise, Antetokounmpo delivered once again.

In doing so, he did what no one outside of Milwaukee believed he could do and brought a success-starved city on the banks of Lake Michigan its first championship in 50 years. ▬▬

ROAD TO
THE TITLE

34

Power Forward

Giannis Antetokounmpo

Loyalty Inside His DNA

By Shams Charania, Eric Nehm, and Sam Amick | December 15, 2020

"One day, he's in 1,000 percent. The next day, he's asking more questions."

That, according to one source with knowledge, describes the ebbs and flows that led to Giannis Antetokounmpo deciding on Tuesday to sign a five-year, $228.2 million supermax contract extension with the Milwaukee Bucks with an opt-out clause in 2025 and a 15 percent trade kicker, sources say. The process leading to the decision, according to sources who spoke to *The Athletic*, consisted of an array of meetings, a hilarious birthday ploy by his teammates to get him to put "pen" to paper, conversations about the Bucks' commitment to roster building after an offseason in which they landed Jrue Holiday and tons of trust by the two-time league MVP in his agent, Alex Saratsis.

"Off the court, about agents and contracts, that's not in my... I'm not focused on that," Antetokounmpo said in the days leading to his announcement. "Not that I don't care about it. Obviously I care about it. It's a very big decision. In my life, probably one of the biggest decisions I'm going to make. I just need my agent to focus on that and I'm going to focus on getting ready Saturday to play the first preseason game."

The largest contract in NBA history keeps Giannis with the Bucks through the 2025-26 season as he joined LeBron James, Anthony Davis and Paul George as players who signed long-term veteran maximum deals this offseason.

Just 13 years ago, Antetokounmpo, then a skinny 13-year-old, started playing basketball competitively for the first time at the behest

In December 2020, Giannis Antetokounmpo signed a five-year, $228.2 million supermax contract extension with the Milwaukee Bucks.

of a coach in Athens, Greece. Doing so helped Antetokounmpo and his older brother, Thanasis, get off the streets where they were selling merchandise to help support their family and into gyms, where they would both blossom into professional basketball players and opened the door for their younger brothers, Kostas and Alex, to eventually become professional basketball players as well. This was not only a major moment for him and the Bucks, but for the NBA, too: Yes, Superstars don't always leave for the large markets. Antetokounmpo proved it — he proved his loyalty to his adopted city and his franchise.

Now, after making four All-NBA teams, four NBA All-Star games and winning Most Valuable Player twice and Defensive Player of the Year, Antetokounmpo has become the league's highest paid player. Here's an inside look at how he came to make that decision.

It was not a straight-forward decision and came with days upon days of deliberating for Antetokounmpo and his inner circle. Sources say he mulled on the decision throughout the past couple of weeks.

The Bucks were able to seal the deal, in part, with a late-in-the-process, crucial sit-down when franchise co-owners Marc Lasry and Wes Edens flew to Chicago on Dec. 12 for a midday meeting with Saratsis.

Throughout the process, the Bucks understood that Antetokounmpo and his inner circle wanted to win first and foremost. Their efforts were placed on selling their franchise cornerstone about their vision for roster building, which is what these meetings consisted of, sources said.

As talks continued in a positive direction, Bucks general manager Jon Horst met with Antetokounmpo's agents, Saratsis and Giorgos Panou of Octagon, on Monday and the sides worked through details on the deal, sources said. Giannis is now guaranteed $256 million over the next six seasons.

While that was a critical meeting in the process, it was not the only one that took place to get the deal done. After spending most of his limited offseason in Greece, Antetokounmpo flew back to Milwaukee on Nov. 29. A few days after landing stateside, the superstar forward met with Saratsis to discuss the supermax extension and figure out how they wanted to proceed.

On Dec. 5, Lasry and Edens joined Antetokounmpo and Saratsis at the superstar's River Hills home for their first in-person discussion about the long-term contract. That is when the Bucks formally presented Antetokounmpo with the five-year, $228.2 million contract, sources said.

Starting in the mid-afternoon, the meeting lasted several hours with Horst also making an appearance to chat with Antetokounmpo about the roster and strategy moving forward. Milwaukee made a series of offseason acquisitions, including trading for Holiday, an All-Star guard and two-way stalwart, to enhance the roster after last season's second-round playoff defeat. After the potential Bogdan Bogdanovic acquisition fell apart, the Bucks' front office had a plan in place. It was prepared for the moment, signing key role players in DJ Augustin, Bobby Portis, Bryn Forbes, Torrey Craig and re-signing Pat Connaughton.

That meeting ended with no resolution. Antetokounmpo took in the information he received from the Bucks and told them he would make a decision once he had time to process things.

Antetokounmpo turned 26 the next day and the Bucks practiced together as a team for the first time during the 2020-21 season following their Saturday off-day. Following that practice, two-time All-Star Khris Middleton informed reporters he had hatched a plan with Connaughton to use the birthday as a way to make sure his teammate of seven seasons knew how the rest of the team felt about Antetokounmpo's future with the Bucks.

"Me and PC (Connaughton) thought the perfect gift to him from all his teammates would be to give him a pen," Middleton said. "So, 19 pens in his locker for his birthday present. I told him those should be some of the best birthday gifts he's ever gotten. So, hopefully he enjoys it and uses it."

While Antetokounmpo's teammates took questions about his future during the team's first four days of media availability, the Bucks' star remained quiet, opting against speaking to reporters. Antetokounmpo would not take questions from reporters until Dec. 9, three days after Middleton's comment, and proceeded to tell reporters contract negotiations were in his agent's capable hands.

On Dec. 10, the Bucks held what was described as a positive and intimate dinner with Antetokounmpo and core players such as Middleton, Brook Lopez and Connaughton as well as Budenholzer and his coaching staff, sources said. It provided everyone the opportunity to discuss the future and build camaraderie entering the new season, another moment for familiar faces to prove to Giannis their commitment toward him — and toward winning.

Even with positive vibes emanating from the dinner as the team got together for their next campaign, there was still no final resolution.

A nightmare scenario avoided

Yet while the Dec. 12 meeting might have ended with clarity on Antetokounmpo's side, Bucks officials were still concerned about the nightmare scenario that might have come next. Were they about to be put in the no-win position that they'd been dreading for years?

Even in the best of times, with both sides building so much trust and goodwill through all these years, this Bucks ownership that took over in 2014 knew the uncomfortable reality that might await. If Antetokounmpo chose to keep his options open, declining the supermax and barreling toward free agency in 2021, then they simply had to consider the merits of moving him. A trade, however heartbreaking it might be given the small-market love affair that had taken place here, was one of the few ways they could avoid the prospect of losing him for nothing (a sign-and-trade next summer would have also been possible).

If the human dynamic wasn't so infinitely important, the shrewd thing to do was to threaten a trade as a way of forcing him to sign. After all, Antetokounmpo had made it clear both publicly and privately that he had no interest in relocating before the end of his contract — at least. Considering Antetokounmpo could expect to receive the same supermax offer from Milwaukee next offseason if he were still in a Bucks jersey, this was the only leverage the incumbents could claim.

But that sort of style belied the nature of their relationship. And so, the Bucks took a more subtle tact. Still, the possibility of the Bucks considering a trade if he hadn't signed the supermax was inevitably real.

The Bucks' plan in that unwelcome scenario, sources say, would have gone something like this...

- After Antetokounmpo declined the supermax, Bucks officials would seek clarity from him and his representative, Saratsis, as to why that choice was made. What made him nervous? What were the biggest factors in his mind? That sort of thing. After a few days of downloading the latest Giannis insight, so to speak, the Bucks would have had a tough choice of their own to make. And Antetokounmpo's message would have mattered a great deal.

- If Antetokounmpo had given some assurance that he was likely to re-sign in Milwaukee as a free agent, perhaps indicating that he'd be back so long as their season didn't end before, say, the conference finals, then sources say Bucks officials likely would have taken their chances and moved ahead with the partnership. But if there were no assurances given, with Antetokounmpo simply stating that he planned on being a free agent and that he'd figure out his future when that time arrived, it's clear the Bucks would have seriously considered whether they needed to take trade calls on him.

So why the wait?

When it comes to Antetokounmpo's concerns, this was a matter of trust and absorbing all of the information.

The Bucks believed that Antetokounmpo had faith in their intentions: Do whatever it takes to build the franchise's first championship team since 1971. But would good intentions be enough in a small market that isn't exactly known for luring free agents?

It seems that was one of the main questions in play. And with so many other suitors from warmer markets waiting to steal him away, the Bucks knew all along that it would be hard to overcome this built-in disadvantage.

"Is it too hard because it's Milwaukee?" one person close to the situation said about these sorts of questions. "Is it easier for him to do all of this in Miami or Dallas or LA?... I think it's a (question of) 'How hard is this?'"

The latest playoff failure had been a brutal reminder that it would never be easy — in Milwaukee or otherwise. After posting the league's best regular season record for a second consecutive campaign, the Bucks — who had lost to Toronto in the 2019 Eastern Conference Finals — had fallen short of their own expectations yet again. And the second-round bouncing by the relentless Miami Heat was just the kind of finish that rival teams hoped would change how Antetokounmpo saw his situation. Especially considering the Finals-or-bust framing of the season that had been so often discussed in the media.

Yet all throughout these past few weeks, the Bucks' confidence was buoyed by the fact that

Antetokounmpo never went dark in terms of communication. In situations such as these, there's nothing more concerning than a good, old-fashioned ghosting. The fact that it didn't happen helped them all sleep a little better at night.

But when it came to his final decision on how he would see the Milwaukee situation, there was this tricky dilemma too: One of the most effective ways of cutting through that market disadvantage — the incumbent star player recruiting fellow stars to come join him — went against Antetokounmpo's nature. For most of his seven NBA seasons, Antetokounmpo had made it clear that he had no interest in being buddy-buddy with stars around the league.

He declined invitations to play with the best of the best during the offseason, most notably a summer workout in 2018 that included three MVPs (LeBron James, Kevin Durant and James Harden). Why join them when you're trying to beat them?

There were no hallway discussions midseason to discuss teaming up free agency — a la Durant and Kyrie Irving before they joined forces in Brooklyn. One of the few exceptions to his reclusive ways — a workout with Kobe Bryant — took place after the late, great Lakers star had retired and thus was seen as a competitive safe space.

All of which made the Bogdanovic situation so concerning for the Bucks last month.

Losing out on a player in free agency was one thing but losing a player whom Antetokounmpo was known to have heavily recruited just weeks before this fork-in-the-road moment for the franchise was quite another. It certainly didn't help matters that it had all been so messy.

The Bucks, of course, believed they had a sign-and-trade lined up with Sacramento for the 28-year-old small forward that came shortly after the Jrue Holiday deal with New Orleans. In terms of the possible ripple effect on Antetokounmpo's choice, sources say there was extreme confidence within the Bucks at the time that their franchise centerpiece would sign the deal, in part, because of the moves that had been made. But then it all fell apart.

Bogdanovic headed for Atlanta. The NBA launched a tampering investigation into the ordeal, in large part, because news of an alleged agreement had leaked via a news outlet nearly five days before the formal start of free agency. The Bucks knew that none of this would help, but it was tough to tell how much it would hurt.

In the end, Antetokounmpo answered the question for them.

The journey to getting Antetokounmpo's signature on the dotted line was filled with far more twists and turns than the Bucks hoped, but in the end, they signed their man and secured the future of their franchise. And Antetokounmpo secured his own future with the only franchise he has ever known.

The Bucks were the team that believed in him enough to take a chance on a rail-skinny 18-year-old playing in small gyms in Greece's second division and then start him by the end of his rookie season when he was just 19. They helped him navigate a country he didn't know and even taught him how to drive a car. They started him the next two seasons as he worked through the growing pains of a young player before handing him the keys to the franchise in his fourth season. They watched him take control and explode into one of the league's brightest stars and take home back-to-back NBA MVPs.

With Antetokounmpo now signed, the Bucks appear set up to contend for years to come. Their star can now do what he has wanted to do all offseason long and focus on the game he loves so much. While the off-the-court distractions might be gone, the pressure to bring a championship to Milwaukee for the first time since '71 has never been greater and Antetokounmpo knows that. In fact, it's the pressure he said he wanted after his rookie season when he tweeted he would not leave the Bucks or the city of Milwaukee until the team was built to a championship level.

That team is here and the time is now.

The Bucks open on Dec. 23 against the Celtics, elated to have their franchise star in place for the next five seasons and intent on helping him attain the one crowning achievement that has eluded him thus far, an NBA championship that won't come easily. ▬▬▬

Breaking Through the Wall

How the Evolution of the Bucks' 'Dunker' Spot Could Be the Key to Playoff Success

By Eric Nehm | May 19, 2021

Bucks coach Mike Budenholzer did not want to talk about it at the start of the season. The Bucks were in the process of making a significant change to their offense in a season with a condensed schedule, limited training camp reps and little practice time. There was no guarantee it would work, so "the dunker" and the team's revamped spacing on offense was not something Budenholzer wanted to discuss at any length publicly in the first few weeks of the season. Now, five months later, Budenholzer references "the dunker" as casually in conversation as he might talk about the 3-point line. It is simply a landmark on the floor, not a classified location worthy of protection with high-security clearance.

While adding a number of new players and figuring out how to integrate Jrue Holiday into a larger role in the team's offensive hierarchy with Giannis Antetokounmpo and Khris Middleton, the Bucks put together the league's fourth-most efficient offense and scored 116.5 points per 100 possessions, an increase of nearly five points from last season (111.9 points per 100 possessions). The entire league scored more efficiently than at any other point in history this season in largely empty arenas, but even noting that qualifier, the Bucks kept pace and performed as a top-five offense despite making changes geared towards making their offense more difficult to guard in the postseason.

"From year to year, they keep the stuff that works well and then they add to it in little ways," said Magic coach Steve Clifford, who took on the Bucks' last season in the first round of the NBA playoffs. "I think that's why Bud is one of the best coaches. He knows his team. He knows what they do well and he stays with those things. And then the things he feels they can fix or make a little bit better, he makes those changes every offseason."

The results were clear, but what did the process look like? Why did the addition of "the dunker" actually work throughout the season? And how might the changes help the Bucks as they head into the playoffs?

After a full season of the Bucks utilizing "the dunker", let's take a closer look at the most important takeaways from what the Bucks did on offense during the regular season.

Weakening the wall

Against the Raptors in 2019 and the Heat in 2020, the respective teams that eliminated the Bucks from back-to-back postseasons effectively walled Antetokounmpo out of the

Under head coach Mike Budenholzer, the Bucks put together the NBA's fourth-most efficient offense during the 2020-21 season, scoring 116.5 points per 100 possessions.

paint by sending extreme help, or "zoning up", when Antetokounmpo had the ball in his hands. This forced him to pass the ball or attempt to drive through the help. It proved to be too difficult and the Bucks could not find an answer. So, one of Budenholzer's biggest priorities in changing the Bucks' offense was making it more difficult for teams to build a wall against Antetokounmpo.

With new spacing, the strategy that once worked against the Bucks was not quite effective. In the Bucks' first matchup against the Heat this season, the Bucks set the NBA single-game record for most made 3-pointers (29). Jimmy Butler did not play in that game (nor any game the Bucks and Heat played this season), but his availability likely would not have changed much about the Heat's defensive strategy in the record-breaking performance because it looked very similar when the Heat and Bucks met four months later in the penultimate game of the regular season.

Bryn Forbes made 45.2 percent of his 3-pointers this season. With a man in "the dunker," Antetokounmpo attacked from the opposite wing instead of the top of the key, which lengthened the distance of Kendrick Nunn's

closeout to Forbes. Nunn got there in time to prevent the catch-and-shoot 3, but Forbes created an easy shot for himself with a pump fake. And for those that might say Forbes will not be good enough on defense to play in a series against the Heat, imagine that same play with Holiday in Forbes' spot. While not the same caliber of knockdown shooter, Holiday still hit 39.2 percent from the 3-point line this season and doesn't need any help getting to the rim.

While this is not all that different from how things worked at the start of the season, the fact that defenses defended it the same in Game 4 as in Game 71 means the changes indeed made it more difficult to build a solid wall.

Slowing down Giannis

Before playing the Bucks, most coaches will talk about the need to slow Antetokounmpo down and keep him away from the rim. The discussion often centers around the need for a team effort and putting more defenders between Antetokounmpo and the basket. That knowledge made the idea of putting another offensive player around the rim in "the dunker" all the more confusing to

Antetokounmpo at the start of the season.

"It makes it harder for me because there's a guy in the paint," Antetokounmpo said following the Bucks' 114-104 win over the Hornets on Apr. 27. "There's a guy in 'the dunker,' so whenever I drive the ball that guy steps up, so now if you're going 100 miles an hour and that guy steps up, it's going to be a charge. But if you're going at your own pace and the guy steps up, you're able to make that pass in the dunker or make that pass in the corner."

When talking about Antetokounmpo getting downhill, the conversation typically focuses on him working in isolation with the ball in his hands. But the same things are true when he is the roll man in a pick-and-roll. In a May match up against Brooklyn, rather than barreling through multiple defenders on a play in the fourth quarter to attempt a dunk to put an exclamation point on a win over one of the top teams in the Eastern Conference, Antetokounmpo short-rolled, surveyed the floor and found DiVincenzo under the basket for an easy look.

"I can't be going 100 miles per hour," Antetokounmpo said. "You have to slow down because if you don't slow down, you're going to get a lot of charges. I think, early in the year ... there was some game where I was going 100 miles an hour and I got a bunch of charges and I was like, 'I can't do this. I gotta slow down.' It took me time to figure it out, but now, if you slow down and you go at your own pace, you can create a lot of assists to the dunker and to the corner."

This season, Antetokounmpo picked up 53 offensive fouls in 61 games, a decrease from the 65 offensive fouls he picked up in 63 games last season. Foul trouble has always been one of the best ways to limit Antetokounmpo and sticking a teammate in "the dunker" has helped the Bucks mitigate that risk by essentially putting a yield sign in the lane for Antetokounmpo on drives.

Changing the help

Following the Bucks' loss to the Raptors in the 2019 Eastern Conference Finals, Antetokounmpo told *The Athletic* he was going to see Marc Gasol double-teaming him as a help defender under the rim every time he got in the gym to work on his game during the offseason. While the Raptors built one of the best initial walls Antetokounmpo had ever encountered in that series, their defense went up another notch because of Gasol's ability to help and double against Antetokounmpo from the backside. Stopping Antetokounmpo doesn't just require a strong wall, but also another layer of defense behind that wall in case Antetokounmpo breaks through the wall.

Traditionally, "the dunker" is occupied by a big man, you know, someone that could dunk with ease on a lob or drop-off pass around the rim. Not with the Bucks though.

"This year, he added more of the dunker space and with guards, with maybe a non-traditional position, which puts a guard in help, puts a guard at the rim," said Celtics coach Brad Stevens, who played Budenholzer and the Bucks in the second round of the 2019 NBA Playoffs. "That (guard) decides whether they're going to help up on drives or whatever the case may be, but it also takes your five man, if he's guarding Lopez, it puts him on the perimeter. Bud's really creative. They're really creative about then recognizing that if you switch that up, to try to have your big closer to the rim, they take advantage of it in other ways."

"Now you're taking a point guard ... and you're asking them to do things over and over within the course of 48 minutes that they haven't done, not just in the NBA, but they've never had to do," Clifford said.

Quarterback Jrue

While adding "the dunker" would have likely made an impact no matter what, Holiday's addition made the changes even more impactful.

"He's good down there," Rockets coach Stephen Silas said. "It's not like he is just going to stand down there and allow you to just go help. As the ball is dribbling to the middle, he is circling underneath and getting little layups. Or as he hits (Giannis), then he's cutting through. Sometimes his defender gets nervous and double teams off him and he gets those quick little layups."

Because of the strange angles, playing well in "the dunker" requires incredible feel. While a player driving to the basket may change directions to get past a defender, the basket remains in front of them at all times. While in "the dunker," a player might initially be behind the backboard or have their back to the basket or need to re-orientate themselves in some way once they catch the ball.

"You're under the defense," 76ers coach Doc Rivers said. "That's all they're trying to do is get someone under the defense and they know if Giannis is going downhill, they got a tough thing. The key is keeping him out of the paint first. The second part is worrying about the dunker."

As the season progressed, Holiday got more comfortable playing in the dunker and began to excel in the space because of his ambidextrousness and incredible court vision. While it is not at all like playing point guard, the skills needed to excel in "the dunker" actually carry over quite nicely.

"He certainly has a knack for finding the open spot," Budenholzer said. "It's some variation of, we call it, working the dunker — cutting, just working behind guys — and Giannis and Khris create so much attention. And he just has a knack. It's been a big part of our evolution. And he embraces it. He can finish down there, which is huge, and then he becomes the quarterback down there. He's certainly got a good feel. When you talk about IQ, that's one of the things you can work on and teach

to some degree, but the timing and understanding some of it just comes inherently."

Will the Bucks break through the wall in the postseason?

The Bucks finished the 2018-19 season fourth and the 2019-20 season eighth in offensive efficiency respectively. They have had great offenses heading into the postseason each of the last two seasons and then teams figured out how to shut down their base actions. This will almost certainly happen again.

Heat coach Erik Spoelstra will have adjustments ready for the Bucks in the first round. He is one of the league's best coaches when it comes to finding ways to slow down an opposing offense, so the Bucks' variability and flexibility will be tested immediately. While the Bucks spent all of last season perfecting the system that came up just short against Toronto in the Eastern Conference finals, they worked to make more significant changes to their offense this season and prepare themselves for this moment.

The organization brought in new players (Holiday, Forbes, Bobby Portis) that can really fill it up offensively. And then they made a new set of rules for their offense to marry that increased offensive talent with a different offensive system after the same things (points in the paint and open 3s) they wanted in the past. There is no denying its success in the regular season.

"I think we just have firepower from everywhere," Holiday said. "Offensively, you can get it one through five. From shooting to penetrating in the paint to ball movement. To Brook, if you want him to have it around the paint, shoot threes or Brook's a load down low. Off the bench. We have Bryn, we have Pat, we have Bobby, all scorers who can really can give it to you any way you want it."

Now, comes the true test: the postseason. ▄▄▄▄

Jrue Holiday

Jrue Holiday and a Mentality Change is What's Different About the Bucks This Year

By Eric Nehm | May 28, 2021

People have only wanted to know one thing about the Bucks since the start of the 2020-21 season: What is actually different about them now?

It's the question people asked when the Bucks dropped their season opener to the Celtics. And when they lost in back-to-back games to the Nets and Lakers to drop to 9-6 through 15 games. And then again when they dropped five straight in February. And once more when the lowly Rockets lit them up for 143 points late in the season. And finally, in the last week of the season, when they opted to beat the Heat to all but guarantee a postseason matchup against the team that eliminated them from the playoffs last season.

As an organization, the Bucks spent the season talking about the adjustments they had made and how they wanted to be different, but as the playoffs began, the answer was still unclear. With a decisive 113-84 victory over the Heat in Miami on Thursday to take a 3-0 lead in their first round series, the Bucks answered the question.

And if their performance was not definitive enough, the first player to step out of the locker room and speak with reporters, P.J. Tucker, tried to make the answer clear.

"We dogs," Tucker said. "That's all we talk about. That's all I ever talk about. We gotta be dogs. People's perceptions of us and what people think in the past, we're erasing all of that. We're coming out every night focused, not shying away from moments. I wasn't here. Jrue wasn't here. Bobby, we got a bunch of new guys in addition to everybody that's been here. We're just bringing that mentality and that's what it's about. Carrying that mentality every game, every possession, every day."

The Bucks lived up to those words on Thursday night. They allowed the Heat to score just 14 points in the first quarter, while they grabbed six

Veteran point guard Jrue Holiday joined the Bucks for the 2020-21 season following seven seasons in New Orleans.

offensive rebounds on the other end of the floor. Even with a double-digit lead for a large majority of the game, the Bucks managed to win all four quarters. They came out with greater intensity than the Heat on their home floor and kept it up for 48 minutes. And while much of the roster is different, Game 3 highlighted the one difference that means more than the rest in the postseason.

"Jrue is the most underrated player in the league, by far," Tucker said. "People don't understand how good he is. I didn't understand how good he was until I played with him. He gets it. And he is the quietest dog you've ever played with in your life. He doesn't say anything, but you know he's there."

On Thursday, there was nothing quiet about Holiday's performance.

The Bucks' starting point guard put up 19 points (on 7-of-10 shooting) and tallied 12 assists, while also making a massive impact defensively. On the night, the Bucks were plus-41 with him on the floor for 34 minutes. Back-to-back MVP Giannis Antetokounmpo (17 points, 17 rebounds and five assists) and Khris Middleton (22 points, 8 rebounds and five assists) were both steady and impactful, but Holiday led the way for the Bucks on Thursday. He was in total control on both ends of the floor and showed why he, among the various new additions, is the biggest difference for the Bucks this season.

Heat coach Erik Spoelstra made a few adjustments before Game 3. He moved Kendrick Nunn out of the starting lineup for Goran Dragic and then shifted Bam Adebayo from Brook Lopez over to Antetokounmpo defensively. Last season,

seeing a bigger and stronger defender like Adebayo instead of a wing like Trevor Ariza would have meant a greater physical beating and a more fortified wall to break through on each drive. Now, Antetokounmpo can just lean on Holiday.

"He's a playmaker," Antetokounmpo said. "When he has the ball in his hands, everybody feels comfortable. Everybody feels like it's a safe place. He's doing a great job finding everybody, finding his teammates, finding me also. But it's an incredible feeling not feeling like all the time that you gotta have the ball, you gotta go through the wall, you gotta make something happen, you gotta find teammates, you gotta go through the pounding. Just gotta play through him."

While Holiday showed off his strength and skill as a scorer on that early possession, his ability to create advantages out of nothing and then pick out the right play shined through as the game progressed.

On a first quarter play, the Heat had a chance to set their defense off of made basket by Tyler Herro. To set the tone for the possession, Nunn tried to pressure Holiday and the Bucks' starting point guard immediately blew by him and the rest of the Heat defense to create what essentially became a fastbreak and an open look for Bryn Forbes, the man who hit six 3-pointers in Game 2.

"He's been doing a great job of mixing it up, whether it's to drive or dish it out," Middleton said. "But he's been doing a great job of reading the defense. He's playing in attack mode, getting down to the paint, trying to get to his spots and then he sees that crowd and he finds the open guy or he gets the hockey assist."

Holiday spent the entire night playing within himself and making the right play. He used his intelligence and his craftiness to set up himself or his teammates, but then, on his 12th and final assist of the night, he reminded everyone he can make plays few others on the planet would think about trying.

Nemanja Bjelica is not a good defender, but that is a left-handed in-and-out dribble into a one-handed lefty skip pass on-time and on-target to the opposite corner for a Pat Connaughton 3 that gave the Bucks a 30-point lead. That is not normal. That is extraordinary.

An equal amount of time could be spent on Holiday's work on the defensive end where his strength, quickness and intelligence have allowed the Bucks to be more versatile and dynamic.

On a first quarter play, Holiday started the possession by picking up Butler in transition and forcing him to kick it out to a teammate. And then instead of watching from the backside as Dewayne Dedmon tried to finish at the rim, Holiday flew in from the corner and contested the shot forcing a miss.

No matter which side of the floor the Bucks were on, Holiday was everywhere and doing everything his team needed in Game 3, which is exactly what Tucker believes makes Holiday so special.

"Consistency," Tucker said. "He's never pressed. He's always going to make the right play. He doesn't care about how many points he's scored. He's not checking the scoreboard. He's worried about not turning the ball over and staying in front of his man and being aggressive on defense and creating for everybody. He's…(pauses, shakes head)…he's really good."

As the Bucks advance in the postseason, Holiday's abilities on both ends of the floor will become even more important. Through three games, his presence on offense has made it more difficult for the Heat to slow down Antetokounmpo and more dangerous for them to keep sending help towards the Bucks' best player. On defense, the Bucks can switch more often and blend defensive schemes in a way they've never previously been able to execute under Budenholzer.

But while Holiday seemingly has an answer for everything the Bucks need on the floor, getting asked how he felt about Tucker's description of him being "the quietest dog" left him a bit flummoxed.

"I don't know what you want me to do with that," Holiday said. "I guess just don't make me mad, really. I don't say much. I don't talk trash, but I get after it and I always will, so I don't know. Maybe it's a little scary messing with a quiet person."

Even with Holiday remaining quiet and calm for now, the Bucks have turned into one of the NBA's scariest teams and the whole league can hear the Bucks barking now. ▬▬▬

22

Small Forward

Khris Middleton

The Bucks' Motto for Khris Middleton, Bucket Getter Extraordinaire: 'Pass it to the Rim'

By Joe Vardon | July 4, 2021

There is a killer among us in the NBA Finals, a low-talking assassin whose method of madness is, in the words of his coach, to "pass the ball to the rim."

Khris Middleton, 29, of Charleston, S.C., is charged in the death of the Atlanta Hawks. He buried them in Game 6 of the Eastern Conference finals with a fury of points in the third quarter seldom seen in any playoff game, tallying 16 in a row and 23 for the quarter in the Bucks' series-clinching, ticket-punching, 118-107 triumph on Saturday night.

Milwaukee may have two stars and a proven complement of role players that put together a body of work over an entire season to reach the Finals for the first time since 1974, but only one of those aces is as of now available. And in the two games the Bucks have won so far without Giannis Antetokounmpo, Middleton performed like the A-lister he has evolved to be, including the game-high 32 points he finished Game 6 with.

"He puts all the weight on his shoulders and doesn't care," marveled Jrue Holiday. "He's like, come on."

There were two games in the Eastern finals that Middleton ended on his own, with a 20-point quarter in each. The other was Game 3, when Giannis was still healthy. The Hawks led for most of that game and were ahead by seven in the fourth quarter when Middleton put the series firmly in the Bucks' grasp with 20 of his 38 points in the final frame. It was the second time this postseason Middleton reached 38 in a game (his playoff career-high), and afterward Giannis said "I trust Khris to death. If Khris asks for the ball, better give him the ball."

It seemed fate and misfortune had pried the series out of Milwaukee's hands, in the cruelest of fashions, when Giannis went down in a heap in the third quarter of Game 4. Images showed the

Khris Middleton stepped up for the Bucks when Giannis Antetokounmpo was injured during the Eastern Conference Finals, leading the Bucks with 32 points in Milwaukee's series-clinching Game 6 win over Atlanta

injury wasn't worse than the original diagnosis of a hyperextended left knee, but it looked bad when it happened, the Hawks tore the Bucks to shreds after Giannis left the game, and of course he hasn't played since.

There were a number of stars and standouts in Game 5 (Brook Lopez' 33 points come to mind, as do the 21 Bobby Portis scored in Giannis' place), but Middleton handed in 26 points, 13 rebounds, and eight assists. It was his seventh double-double of the postseason — he only had six career double-doubles in the playoffs coming into this year.

The Hawks had ample reason for optimism heading into Game 6, starting with the return of their top talent, Trae Young, from the bruised right foot that cost him two games. The other — since Feb. 21, the Hawks' 23 wins at home were tied for the most in the league. The Bucks had also shown incapable for much of the series to keep their focus from game to game; after an excellent performance in Game 5 without Giannis, they were ripe for a letdown and a dramatic Game 7 to follow.

The Hawks, as it turned out, didn't get a healthy Trae Young. He looked slow and tentative and shot 4-of-17. But at halftime, the score was Bucks 47, Hawks 43, in large part because Middleton (and to a slightly lesser extent, Holiday) had been pretty terrible. Middleton missed all three shots he took in the second quarter and committed four of his six turnovers for the half, which triggered coach Mike Budenholzer to remind Middleton to, you know, instead of throwing the ball away on these bad passes, just pass the ball to the rim.

"Baskets," Budenholzer explained. "You know, he's a bucket-getter. He's just got such a great overall package, and I think he's just an underrated playmaker. He's an underrated passer. But it's all built off him just being a great, great shooter. So any time he can shoot, I think he's got the ultimate green light."

Middleton whiffed on the Bucks' first shot of the half. The Hawks' Kevin Huerter had a clean look at a 3 on the ensuing possession that would have given them their first lead. And then Middleton clipped their wings.

It started with a hard-charging layup with 11:07 to go in the period. Then a 3. And another. He was fouled on a short jumper, making that shot and the free throw. Then he drained a 17-footer. By this point, with still 9:08 remaining in the third, the Bucks' lead jumped to 60-45. If you're keeping track, Middleton had scored 13 unanswered. He knocked down another 25-footer for 16 consecutive points on Milwaukee's behalf, all by himself, and his 21st, 22nd, and 23rd points of the quarter came on yet another 3, with 2:30 left, for an 81-66 advantage.

"Just want to win, that's all it is," Middleton said. "I don't care how many points I have. Stats go out the window. Even though I had a great third quarter, I told Jrue I was struggling. I just want to win, you've got to get the ball and make something happen because right now I just don't have it. That's what it's about, everybody on this team, we don't care about who has the ball, who scores, who does this and that. We just do what it takes to win and that's all you want."

Like Middleton, Holiday is a member of the USA men's basketball team that's headed to Tokyo next month. Holiday finished right behind Middleton Saturday with 27 points, nine boards and nine assists, and because of their efforts, they

Khris Middleton's 23 points in the third quarter of Game 6 of the Eastern Conference Finals were the third-most in any quarter of any postseason game in the last 25 years.

all but guaranteed that they will miss the entirety of Team USA's training camp in Las Vegas that starts Tuesday — the same day as Game 1 of the Finals in Phoenix.

Middleton went cold in the fourth quarter and the Hawks got as close as six after trailing by 22, but it was what he did in the third that changed the game and effectively ended the series. When it was over, ESPN's Mark Schwartz told Middleton that his 23 points in the third were the third-most in any quarter of any postseason game in the last 25 years, trailing only Allen Iverson and Damian Lillard (his eventual Team USA teammate).

"It's a cool stat," Middleton replied. "I guess I would say that it would only mean something if we win. Whatever it takes to win, that's it."

Middleton is a bit of a low talker, and could barely be heard in the din of the Bucks' makeshift press conference area inside State Farm Arena, where the acoustics are terrible and the air conditioning hums. He's not one to get overly excited, especially about something he's done, anyway.

Holiday was a little more effusive in his praise.

"The way that he plays and scoring 20 points in multiple quarters of multiple games is something that I can tell my kid that I've witnessed, and when I go back and watch the film, I can tell them I was out there fighting with him," Holiday said.

In an NBA postseason dominated by injuries to stars, the two-time MVP hurting his knee did not sink the Bucks. All eyes will be on Giannis and his recovering knee between now and Game 1 against the Suns, and of course for every day beyond that, whether he's played or not, until the Finals are over.

There are many days ahead and empty column inches to fill with Giannis speculation, and how his absence or presence affects the Bucks in the Finals. For this morning, though, they're an organization that deserves to celebrate getting that far in the first place, with the knowledge that, when healthy, they really do have two players capable of changing the complexion of any game, and any series.

"Khris is the heart of this team," Holiday said. "I feel like Giannis is the soul of this team, and without them, man, we really wouldn't be here." ▬▬▬

The AntetokounBros

The Antetokounmpo Brothers Share the Court, Giannis Calls It: 'The Best Moment We've Ever Had in the NBA'

By Eric Nehm | April 1, 2021

With just over a minute remaining in the Milwaukee Bucks' 112-97 win over the Los Angeles Lakers on Wednesday, it was time for Thanasis Antetokounmpo to do something his younger brother, Giannis Antetokounmpo, was unwilling to do when he had the chance just a minute earlier: bully their little brother, Kostas.

With the ball in his hands late in one of the Bucks' final offensive possessions, Thanasis, 28, initiated a pick-and-roll and got Kostas Antetokounmpo, 23, to switch off of his man and onto him. With Kostas covering him on the switch, Thanasis put the ball in between the legs and dribbled out to the 3-point line on the right wing. Kostas didn't stick close enough to him though, and Thanasis took one more dribble to set up a stepback 3. Kostas read the move, likely because he had seen it hundreds of times during various offseason workouts with his older brother, and contested it well, but it didn't matter.

Thanasis rose up just high enough and nailed the 3 over Kostas' outstretched right arm.

"I don't know, Thanasis is just ruthless, man," Giannis joked after the game. "Went in, had the stepback on his little brother. Come on, man. How can you do that to your little brother? I had the opportunity to do the same, but I didn't."

By that point, Giannis, 25, could only watch from the sidelines as his brothers went head-to-head, but he had been on the floor with both of his brothers for the first time in his career just moments earlier. For 52 seconds, Giannis, Kostas, and Thanasis shared the court, becoming just the second trio of brothers to share the floor in an NBA game.

The first trio of brothers to accomplish the feat was the Holiday brothers — Aaron, Jrue, Justin — on Dec. 28, 2019, when all three shared the floor during the third quarter of a 120-98 Pelicans win over the Pacers. (After Wednesday's game, Jrue Holiday shared that he thought Thanasis was right to bully Kostas with the stepback 3: "As you should, that's little brother.")

Being the second trio of brothers to accomplish the feat, however, did not make the moment any less special.

Thanasis Antetokounmpo looks toward his brother Giannis Antetokounmpo during a March 29, 2021, game between the Bucks and Los Angeles Clippers in Los Angeles.

"This moment today is probably my favorite moment I've had so far in the NBA," Giannis said after putting up 25 points and 10 rebounds in the win. "You can never have a feeling like this, no matter what you do. You win a game with a buzzer beater, you score 50, you score 40 — like, it does not frickin' matter.

"This moment, just seeing the guys that I grew up with, and we slept in the same bed, and we were looking at the ceiling and imagining if we were ever going to play in the NBA, if we were ever going to make it and just being on the same court while our mom is having her phone and videotaping the whole thing — I think it's priceless, and nobody can take this away from us. I think this is the best moment we've ever had in the NBA."

By now the family's story is well-known, but here is a quick recap for those reading it for the first time.

In total, there are five Antetokounmpo brothers. Francis, 32, was the firstborn son of Veronika and Charles Antetokounmpo in 1988. When Veronika and Charles decided to leave Lagos, Nigeria and look for new opportunities in Greece in 1991, Francis stayed in Lagos to be raised by his grandparents. In 1992, Thanasis was born in Athens, Greece.

Giannis, Kostas and Alex, their 19-year-brother currently playing professionally for Spanish club UCAM Murcia, were all born in Athens as well, where the family lived for two decades until Giannis was discovered by professional scouts and drafted by the Bucks with the 15th overall pick in the 2013 NBA Draft. Giannis made his way to the United States by himself that summer and lived in Milwaukee alone for a few months until the proper paperwork came through and Charles, Veronika, Kostas and Alex were able to join him stateside. (Thanasis was pursuing his dream and playing professionally first in the Greek second division and then in the G League with the Delaware 87ers during this time.)

From there, Giannis developed from an intriguing rookie to an NBA All-Star to a two-time NBA MVP. And the brothers who lived with him in Greece all pursued the same dream.

After his first stint in the NBA with the Knicks in 2016 did not work out, Thanasis continued his professional career overseas for three years until the Bucks signed him as a free agent in July 2019.

Kostas took a more traditional route. He went to Dominican High School in Whitefish Bay, a northern suburb of Milwaukee, for two years before moving on to the University of Dayton for two years. He was selected with the final pick of the 2018 NBA Draft and traded to the Mavericks, who waived him after one season. The Lakers swooped in to sign him to a two-way contract before the 2019-20 NBA season. Last year, Kostas became the first Greek-born player to win an NBA championship.

And after accomplishing all of that, the three brothers finally got the chance to share an NBA floor together on Wednesday.

"It's amazing, man," Giannis said. "It's been a long, long journey to be able to have the three of us be in the same NBA court, man. It's amazing. Our mom is right there watching. You can never ask for anything better. We're representing our father in the right way. We're doing it with a smile on our face. We're try to improve every single day, and this was always our dream. Just being able to take a moment and realize that we accomplished it, it's amazing. We gotta keep getting better, keep working on our game and hopefully moments like this, like tonight, can happen again."

Not only was this the first time all three brothers got on the floor together; this was the first time Giannis got to play against one of his brothers in the NBA. Giannis and Thanasis have been

Thanasis Antetokounmpo (left) signed with Milwaukee in July 2019, joining his brother Giannis, bringing endless energy and enthusiasm to the Bucks' roster.

together on the Bucks for the last two seasons, so they never got the chance to compete against each other, and while Kostas has suited up against the Bucks twice in the past — once with the Mavericks and once with the Lakers — he had not gotten into the game until Wednesday.

After the game, Giannis admitted he didn't quite know how to react.

"I'm just focused on the game, try to have fun, try to help my team win but did not see Kostas taking his warmup and getting to enter the game," Giannis said. "But when I looked, I saw that he was standing up. I don't remember who told me, but somebody told me, 'Your brother is about to go in the game.' I was obviously happy. I knew that was one opportunity for me to play against him. I've seen Jrue and his brother play in the past in the same game, but I never thought about it."

"Usually when I think about it, it's whenever we play the Lakers. Whenever we come over here,

I'm like, "Oh, my brother is on the opposite team. Who knows, I might play against him. And what if I play against him? What am I going to do? How am I going to guard him? Am I going to guard him? I know his moves. I know his weaknesses, stuff like that. But at the end of the day, when the game starts, I just try to focus on what I have to do to help my team win, but in the last minute and a half, I had the opportunity to just have fun and enjoy those few seconds that I played against him that we all played together."

Now the Antetokounmpo brothers just need their youngest brother Alex to get to the NBA, so they can become the first family in NBA history to have four brothers share the floor together. It seems unlikely at the moment, but so were three brothers who shared the same bed in Athens, Greece, making their way to the NBA and playing in the same game. It might not be wise to count out the Antetokounmpo family. ▬▬▬

Brook Lopez

How 'Frasier' Explains Why Brook Lopez and Mike Budenholzer's Eclectic Partnership Drives the Bucks' Defense

By Eric Nehm | June 2, 2021

Shortly after the Bucks eliminated the Heat from the playoffs, Bucks coach Mike Budenholzer stepped to the virtual dais and spoke with reporters. He talked about all the reasons his team was able to flip the script and eliminate the Heat 264 days after the Heat had done the exact same thing to them during the 2020 postseason, but one sentence stuck out among the rest.

"Brook has been really good this series," Budenholzer said.

Brook Lopez was not the only player Budenholzer praised after the victory. Budenholzer spoke at length about Giannis Antetokounmpo's special skill set and why it allowed him to impact the series defensively. He discussed the poise and calm provided by Khris Middleton and Jrue Holiday, as well as the knockdown shooting of Bryn Forbes. He discussed all of the players that made an impact in the Bucks sweep of the Heat, but Lopez was the lone player that Budenholzer gave a final sentence to summarize the performance and he was right.

Lopez was really good against the Heat.

He increased his regular-season scoring and rebounding averages to 15.8 points and 6.8 rebounds per game by giving the Bucks a presence down low and "owning the paint," as the team described throughout the series. On defense, he covered Bam Adebayo and limited the Heat's All-Star center to 15.5 points per game on 45.5-percent shooting and also helped off of Adebayo to make it difficult on the rest of the Heat roster any time they came near the paint. It left Adebayo and the Heat looking for answers offensively that they just did not have.

Brook Lopez dunks over Miami Heat forward Jimmy Butler and center Bam Adebayo during the first round of the 2021 NBA playoffs.

A year after the organization's greatest postseason disappointment in decades, the Bucks managed a small measure of revenge by beating the team that eliminated them earlier than anybody expected last postseason. At the center of it all was the odd couple of Budenholzer and Lopez.

Before the Bucks signed him on July 8, 2018, Lopez was known only for his offense and quirky personality. As the Warriors built a dynasty with 6-foot-6 Draymond Green closing out games at center, the league became more enamored with small-ball lineups and mobile big men. So, when the Bucks signed Lopez, a 7-foot, 280-pound center, Budenholzer did not believe the Bucks had just signed an All-Defensive center.

"I'll stop you, no, the answer is no," Bucks coach Mike Budenholzer said. "I had no idea ... It's been a great revelation.

"I was really excited about the shooting and the spacing and he's incredibly talented offensively and I must have just missed it, I don't know," Budenholzer said. "I had no idea the defender, the impact he was going to have on our team."

By the time the Bucks convened for training camp at the end of September, Budenholzer had devised a defensive strategy that played to his big man's stature. Lopez stuck around the rim and tried to contest as many shots as possible, while then-point guard Eric Bledsoe fought over the top of screens and tried to force offensive players toward Lopez. The Bucks' wings, led by Antetokounmpo and Middleton, filled in the cracks around the rest of the floor and flew around to help out and keep teams from getting to the rim.

After 20 games, the Bucks were sixth in defensive efficiency. Through 41 games, they had moved up to third. And by the end of the season, they were the league's best defense, holding opponents to 104.9 points per 100 possessions. As the season progressed, Lopez showed that he was not a defensive liability, but rather one of his team's best defenders.

And it wasn't just that Lopez could get the job done; he reveled in the work of being a great defender and leading a great defensive team. As covered in this space at the end of the 2019-20 season, Lopez took what he did in his first season with the Bucks and then studied the Bucks' scheme (and the NBA's rulebook) to figure out all the small tricks he needed to become one of the league's best defensive players in his second season in Milwaukee. He got even better, which helped the Bucks get even better, and eventually earned him a spot on the NBA's All-Defensive Second Team.

But all of that came crashing down against the Heat in last year's playoffs.

Goran Dragic and Tyler Herro rained floaters down over the top of Lopez's head. Jimmy Butler repeatedly stopped short of Lopez and knocked down pull-up jumpers, which Lopez could not contest. Kelly Olynyk picked-and-popped his way to open 3-pointers with Lopez stuck in a help position. Whatever was working for the Bucks defensively in the last two seasons had been solved and they needed to make changes. That started with Lopez doing new and different things.

The Bucks spent the 2020-21 season trying new things on defense and that is how Lopez succinctly and respectfully described one of the team's most epic failed experiments.

While the Bucks were initially attracted to Brook Lopez's shooting prowess, the center's defensive talent has been a key revelation on the team's path to an NBA title.

"I mean, I was supposed to switch onto (T.J.) McConnell and I didn't, so I messed up my coverage there," Lopez told reporters following the Bucks' 140-113 victory over the Pacers on March 22. "Again, I thought I saw something and I tried to; we talked about it once when you guys saw on the court, and we talked about it on the sideline, and it is what it is. We're all moving forward and learning, and it's something that happened in the game. It's a typical Brook-Bud interaction."

Instead of just taking Lopez's recounting of the situation, let's take a closer look.

Halfway through the third quarter, the Pacers initiated a set that started with two-time All-Star Domantas Sabonis setting a screen for McConnell. While it might have looked like a normal pick-and-roll initially, it was actually Spain action, which is a pick-and-roll action that involves a second screener setting a pick for the screener in the initial pick-and-roll.

And a play that confused the Bucks throughout the regular season.

Not only did the Bucks screw up a switch on a third quarter possession, but they also gave up an offensive rebound after Lopez swatted at a rebound to get it away from the rim.

That led to Budenholzer yelling at Lopez — and Lopez yelling right back at Budenholzer as the play continued. Eventually, Pacers guard Justin Holiday made a 3, and as Lopez made his way down the floor for the Bucks' offensive possession, he and Budenholzer continued their lively discussion.

For the next 10 minutes, through gameplay, a timeout, a stoppage in play and Lopez getting subbed out of the game, they kept talking. Lopez argued his point of view, while Budenholzer argued right back. After some animated discussion, Lopez searched out assistant coaches to bring into the conversation, but eventually ended up sitting right next to Budenholzer to argue some more. At times, the discussion was animated. Other times, it was calm, but it kept going as both explained their separate points of view.

"It wasn't about the defensive rebound," Lopez said. "It was about the initial pick-and-roll and we were all switching and I thought I saw something myself, so Bud and I talked about it in the typical way we tend to talk about things (laughs)."

While most coaches might not entertain this type of pushback from most players, Budenholzer understands that he and Lopez are wired the same way. Both are obsessed with getting better defensively and feel strongly about how to best accomplish the goal, which means they often disagree. If Budenholzer does not satisfy Lopez's intellectual curiosity, Lopez will question it. His questions are not challenges to Budenholzer's authority, but rather philosophical inquiries about the Bucks' defense they both care about deeply.

And those inquiries have turned into interactions Budenholzer loves so much that when asked about the argument he had with Lopez a few days after it happened, as well as the rest of the arguments they've had over the last three seasons, Budenholzer got emotional and reflected on their relationship:

"One of my absolute favorite things about coaching the Milwaukee Bucks and coaching Brook. He is incredible. And I'm so appreciative of what he does defensively. It's just insane how good he is. So, I occasionally tell him that, but not very often because then I would be on the wrong side when we start to argue and fight, so I don't want him to know that I think he's amazing.

"In all honesty, the genuine passion for the defense and for being great and what we want to do, and he and I joke about us both being like a couple of volcanoes. It's been, there's been so many good things coaching here the last few years, but coaching Brook, it's just — and his ability to lighten the mood in a film session. I could be talking or we could be working on or discussing something else and he can interject an opinion or come to throw a lifeline to someone else and sometimes use humor, it's just been incredibly important. And for me as a head coach, you need those guys in a locker room. You need that kind of conversation and sometimes you disagree on things and then you gotta work through it. It's definitely been one of the beautiful things of Brook and I here the last couple of years."

While that night in March looked ugly, Lopez was ready when he needed to switch and move his feet against the Heat.

Time and time again, Heat ballhandlers turned the corner against their primary defender and immediately saw Lopez. Rather than waiting by the rim, Lopez jumped out of the lane and pressured the Heat guards into picking up their dribble or abandoning their drive altogether.

And in the moments Adebayo would cut to the open space, Lopez recovered back to his area and contested the shot. Nothing was easy for the Heat and that was largely because Lopez had changed in such a way that he was ready to do something new and different in the postseason.

When Bucks general manager Jon Horst traded for P.J. Tucker on March 19, a portion of the Bucks fanbase believed their team had found their new postseason closer. After watching Tucker excel with the Rockets as a small-ball center, there was a belief that the Bucks' best postseason lineups would feature Tucker instead of Lopez as the Bucks embraced a switchy, small-ball unit that could compete against the league's best in the postseason.

As so often happens, Lopez's brain went in a different direction. A very different direction. His brain went to "Frasier."

For those uninitiated, "Frasier" was an American television sitcom that continued the story of psychiatrist Frasier Crane, one of the recurring characters on "Cheers," as he left Boston and returned home to Seattle to start a new career as a radio show host and reconnect with his father and brother. In the pilot episode, which debuted on Sept. 16, 1993, Crane finds out his father is no longer capable of living alone and needs to move into Crane's apartment, which triggers a conversation about the apartment's interior decor.

Somehow, this was the only thing that could come to mind when Lopez thought about the Bucks adding Tucker.

"It kind of reminds me of this 'Frasier' quote from early in the series about eclectic design," Lopez said on March 23, just five days after the Bucks added Tucker. "He's talking about the furniture in his apartment. It's a lot of different high-end pieces of furniture and he talks about how with eclectic design if it's all truly really nice and high-quality and good-looking, it will all match and go together, and I guess my mind went right there.

"It's kind of the same way with great defenders, I think. Obviously, they're all going to find a way to work together. I think it's going to work pretty quickly together and be natural."

And sure enough. Tucker and Lopez shared the floor together regularly during the Heat series and likely will need to do so again in the second round in a potential matchup against the Nets. While doing things in a slightly different way with slightly different pieces around him, Lopez shined defensively in the first round, but he and the Bucks will need to be able to embrace a flexible defensive philosophy with a slightly different set of rules in the second round to advance once again.

So, "Frasier" it is?

"I actually do like 'Frasier,'" Budenholzer said. "I probably like episodes early, middle, late. I'm good with Frasier, but I'm not sure Frasier and Brook and I have crossed paths yet, so down the road. We have more to look forward to."

Just another topic for them to talk about during their "typical Brook-Bud interactions" that have formed a bond that is anything but typical. ▬▬

9

Bobby Portis

Fan Favorite Bobby Portis Pays Off for Bucks, GM Jon Horst

By Joe Vardon | July 2, 2021

The playoffs are a typically excruciating time for the front-office executives whose teams compete in them. There's nothing much they can do, other than watch. They can't make any trades, or call someone up from the G League, or sign a free agent.

As the games unfold and series unwind, these team presidents and general managers are either treated to proof that their months and years of roster construction have paid off, or they watch in agony as the big moves they thought they made don't pan out in the most important moments. To the degree these men can impact a playoff game at all, the differences they made were the free agents they signed and trades they pulled off during the previous offseason, or at the trade deadline, or when the buyout market heated up.

The Bucks' general manager, Jon Horst, had one of those moments in Game 5 of the Eastern Conference finals. Milwaukee beat the Atlanta Hawks 123-112 to take a 3-2 series lead, placing

them one win from the Finals, in no small part due to the most consequential maneuvers he made in November, a month before the season even began. And one was to correct a colossal mistake.

The point guard Horst traded for, Jrue Holiday, was brilliant in that Game 5 with 25 points and 13 assists. And the forward he signed after an attempted trade blew up in his face, well, he made his first career playoff start and finished with a career-best 22 points and eight rebounds, all in place of the injured two-time MVP Giannis Antetokounmpo.

That man's name is Bobby Portis. He is inarguably a fan favorite in Milwaukee, so much so that the packed Fiserv Forum echoes his name in mesmerizing, thunderous "Bobb-y, Bobb-y" chants. Portis almost certainly wouldn't even be a Buck right now had the player Horst tried to trade for ended up in Milwaukee.

And here's what makes this whole storyline so juicy: that player is Bogdan Bogdanovic, who's

Acquired as a free agent during an eventful November for the Bucks front office, Bobby Portis has emerged as a fan favorite, bringing depth and athleticism to Milwaukee's roster.

starting and scoring for the Hawks in this series. The Bucks won Game 5 behind a career night from their consolation prize.

After many of us went to bed one night in mid-November, it was reported that Horst had swung two massive, franchise-altering trades. First, he moved Eric Bledsoe, George Hill, three first-round picks and two future pick swaps to the Pelicans for Holiday, a past All-Star and upgrade over Bledsoe. Then, he agreed to the framework for a sign-and-trade deal with the Sacramento Kings for Bogdanovic. But there was a catch or two, and they turned out to be massive.

One, Bogdanovic was entering his restricted free agency. Two, he was not yet a restricted free agent, so by league rule the Kings and Bucks could not have agreed to that trade yet. And three, because such agreements go on secretly all the time before the legal period begins, the deal blew up because it was leaked to the media. The NBA opened an investigation, which effectively canceled the trade — because if Bogdanovic agreed to it, it would be considered proof of tampering on the part of the Bucks — and the league ended up taking a 2022 second-round pick away from Milwaukee anyway.

As embarrassing and disappointing as the whole ordeal was, it came at a particularly sensitive time in Bucks' history, as Horst and team ownership was trying to convince Giannis to sign a supermax extension.

About a week after the Bogdanovic deal went sideways, Horst recovered by signing Portis to a two-year, $7.4 million contract through free agency. Portis is nowhere near the floor spacer Bogdanovic is, but he brought size and athleticism to the Bucks' bench, primarily as Giannis' backup. And in this series, Portis has not only made Horst look really smart, but has endeared himself to the thousands of Milwaukeeans who cram into Fiserv Forum for these games.

After taking three DNPs in the second round against Brooklyn, Portis has scored over 10 points in three of the five games against the Hawks. Those boisterous "Bobb-y" chants began in earnest during a 34-point blowout in Game 2, and of course, they returned with Portis starting and dominating with Giannis out. He took 20 shots (!) and added three steals. And the crowd adored him, for every corner 3, steal and dunk, or flexing of muscles and gesturing to the fans to "let's go!"

"Milwaukee's a tough city," Portis said. "You know, some people at the start of the season — they were telling us all about the city and how tough it is to live here and things like that, and you know, the city goes through a lot. So, when they see somebody that gives his all and works hard, because it's a blue-collar city and I'm a blue-collar player, I'm going to make the shots — whether they are going in or not, I still give my all to the team 100 percent, for the name in front of the jersey and they love players like that."

The most points Portis had ever scored in a playoff game prior to Game 5 was his first, back on April 16, 2017, when he scored 19 for the Bulls. His career has taken lots of dips and wrong turns. He punched a teammate and was suspended eight games, was relegated to the G League, traded to the Wizards, and spent a season in New York. He said signing with the Bucks "was one of the best decisions for my career."

"Finally found peace, man," Portis said. "I'm at

Center Bobby Portis scores as Phoenix Suns guard Cameron Payne, bottom, looks on during Game 2 of the NBA Finals.

peace with myself and at peace in my life and at peace with everything going on around."

Horst's trade for Holiday was necessary. The Bucks clearly needed a third scorer and a more dynamic player at the top of the offense. Holiday is much bigger than Bledsoe, too, which makes him more versatile on defense. League observers still contend the Bucks are trying to recover from allowing Malcolm Brogdon to leave to the Pacers (via a sign and trade) instead of paying him in 2019. The Brogdon deal is typically laid at the feet of Bucks ownership, instead of Horst, for not wanting to pay into the luxury tax, but Horst was nonetheless the general manager when it happened. Acquiring Holiday (an All-NBA defender) wasn't just to upgrade from Bledsoe, it was to try and finally solve the hole created by not keeping the 2016-17 Rookie of the Year.

"I'm grateful for the Bucks," Holiday said. "I'm blessed for them to come and grab me the way that they did and to be put in this position. This is my first conference finals ever. So I'm just happy and blessed to be here. I want to make the most of it, take advantage of it."

If Bogdanovic denies the Bucks a trip to the Finals, it will be the bitterest of pills to try and wash down with Miller Lite here. And it could still happen. Bogdanovic's balky knee is feeling better, and in the last two games he's scored 20 and (in Game 5) 28 points. He drained seven 3s on Thursday.

But for the Bucks and Horst, Bogdanovic's big night wasn't enough to overcome Holiday and Portis. The Hawks need to win Game 6 on their home court just to keep this series alive, and if so, Game 7 is back at Fiserv, where the Bucks have lost just once this postseason, Portis is adored, Holiday is thrilled to play and the GM is happy to have them both. ▬▬

P.J. Tucker

Has P.J. Tucker Finally Found What he has Been Looking for with the Milwaukee Bucks?

By Eric Nehm | July 5, 2021

For seven games in the Eastern Conference semifinals, P.J. Tucker went toe-to-toe with Nets forward Kevin Durant.

To be clear, he did not go basket-for-basket; Tucker versus Durant wasn't a scoring duel. Tucker put everything he had into his defensive effort and making it as tough as possible for Durant to score in the Bucks' second-round series.

The Bucks' wing first met Durant on a University of Texas recruiting trip where Tucker told then-head coach Rick Barnes that Durant is going to be "the best player I've ever seen in my life," so he knew what the job required. And he gave everything to that matchup, so much so that he joked that he exerted so much energy on defense that he told his teammates "good luck" in regards to what they'd get out of him on offense in the series.

After seven games though, despite mammoth numbers from Durant, the Bucks came out on top with an overtime victory in Game 7 in Brooklyn. When asked to consider the journey that led him to that place, to that duel with Durant in the playoffs, Tucker gave a 30-second answer about his journey, but then took an extra second to cap his answer with a three-word sentence:

"I'm just happy."

The life of an NBA player is focused on wins and losses, victory and defeat, accomplishment and failure. It is black and white. Players either make the shot or they miss the shot. The team either overcomes an obstacle or falls short of a goal. The human existence that exists in between those binary feelings often goes unnoticed and undiscussed as games are decided.

So, it was interesting to hear a player so hyper-focused on an individual battle and getting a win speaking on the more existential nature of being a professional athlete. With so much of a player's life defined by wins and losses that may not be totally

Forward P.J. Tucker scores during Game 1 of the NBA Finals as Phoenix Suns players Jae Crowder and Mikal Bridges look on.

in his control, happiness must be difficult to find.

"It's impossible," Tucker told The Athletic in an exclusive interview between Games 3 and 4 of the Eastern Conference finals. "It is. It really is. It's thee impossible."

"To be able to go through all the stuff that you go through in seasons with teams and front offices and all the different things, the twists and turns a career has. To be able to get to that point where you go through some tough, dark times, things that fall apart, to finding your footing back at somewhere you want to be, like there are so many different variables, man, to actually get back to a place with yourself that you can actually say, 'You know what, I'm just enjoying this and happy because I've seen the other side and been there and know how that feels to be in that place.' It's unimaginable. Like I said, it's almost impossible in this day."

For Tucker, going against Durant was the reward for everything he had gone through in the last season.

"I thought about the stuff I was doing with Houston this year, this season has just been a long year for me," Tucker said. "To go from being a top team in the West to falling apart instantly and being the last one left (in Houston) and everything I went through with that, the transition, it was just a lot this season.

"That battle with KD was just like that big, heavyweight fight. Just night after night, giving it all and being exhausted and just fighting and fighting and just to come out on top of that after going through all of that, plus that (matchup), that was that moment. That was that, you fought all night and then at the end of the day, you just

want to be happy."

While things are going well for Tucker and the Bucks on the eve of Game 1 of the NBA Finals, Tucker took a circuitous journey to Milwaukee.

Things went downhill for the Rockets starting in the NBA bubble. After beating Chris Paul and the Oklahoma City Thunder in the first round of the 2020 playoffs, the Rockets took Game 1 against the Los Angeles Lakers in a game Tucker started at center and played 35 minutes. From there, everything fell apart. The Rockets lost the next four games and then head coach Mike D'Antoni and the Rockets parted ways, essentially on the plane ride out of the bubble, on Sep. 15, 2020. One month later, general manager Daryl Morey resigned. Two weeks later, the organization named Stephen Silas head coach.

In a two-month span, the Rockets went from stumbling onto a fun, small-ball, switch-heavy approach with Tucker in a key role at center to a franchise devoid of direction, trying to find the next step forward. They quickly found their direction, but it was moving in the opposite one Tucker might have hoped.

On Nov. 22, the team traded Robert Covington, the switchy wing with length and strength who helped fuel the Rockets' small-ball starting unit. Two days later, Houston completed a sign-and-trade for Christian Wood, a prized free-agent forward, albeit young and inexperienced. Three days later, they sent Austin Rivers out the door. And then, on Dec. 2, the team swapped Russell Westbrook for John Wall, who had not played an NBA game since Dec. 26, 2018.

Harden, Tucker and Eric Gordon were the

P.J. Tucker defends Kevin Durant during the first half of Game 7 against the Brooklyn Nets, the culmination of a series-long battle.

only main contributors left on the roster from the day Tucker signed with the Rockets on July 6, 2017, just 10 days after the Rockets had traded for Paul. And then Harden forced his way out of town. On Jan. 14, the Rockets were 4-6 when the Nets traded for Harden. In the weeks after he left, the Rockets fought hard and managed to claw their way to a winning record at 10-9, but then they dropped 20 straight games and those losses weighed on Tucker, who the Bucks often describe as a "winning player," more than anyone else. While he was watching Paul find success in Phoenix and Harden join a super team in Brooklyn, Tucker was marooned in Houston with one of the league's worst teams.

"I was low," Tucker said. "It was low. I did not enjoy that. I gave up so much. Like players put that together, guys getting together, talking, and

I left a great situation I was in Toronto, other situations I had, other deals, other offers. I left a lot on the table to be a part of that, so in the end, to be last and be there, to have to deal with what I dealt with them leaving as well, that was, I don't know if it was the lowest (point in my career), but it was low. It wasn't good."

Following the All-Star break, the Rockets decided to make Tucker inactive for games as they assessed the situation and tried to find a trade partner. He sat out for five games before the Rockets eventually found a deal with Milwaukee. Bucks general manager Jon Horst gave up D.J. Wilson and D.J. Augustin, while creatively moving picks around to let the Rockets move into the first round with the Bucks' 2021 draft pick (eventually No. 24 in the 2021 NBA Draft) while the Bucks moved back to the start of the second round (eventually the No. 31 pick).

The Bucks sat Tucker for 10 games shortly after he joined them to heal a left calf strain that Tucker later revealed he had been playing through with the Rockets in order to help win games, but for Milwaukee, that was not necessary. The Bucks were not focused on winning regular-season games this season. They wanted Tucker to be ready for the postseason, where the Bucks knew they would need his toughness and ability to switch defensively to give opponents different defensive looks.

"His whole career, he's been a guy that guards one through five," Bucks star Khris Middleton said at NBA Finals media day Monday. "So to have him on our team to give us the confidence to throw those different lineups out there and rely on him in a lot of different situations, it's been great."

As soon as the Bucks hit the postseason, Tucker's tenacity gave the Bucks an edge they had lacked in the previous two postseasons. In the first round, it was Tucker who split time on Heat star Jimmy Butler with Giannis Antetokounmpo and told the world that this Bucks roster is full of "dogs," which has turned into a rallying cry this postseason.

And then in the second round, Tucker lived his dream and spent an entire playoff series "guarding the best player in the world," which eventually propelled the Bucks to the Eastern Conference finals for the second time in three seasons. Then, after beating the two other teams Tucker thought about wanting to get traded to in the first two rounds, the Bucks started off the third round with a Game 1 loss to the lower-seeded Atlanta Hawks, who got a career performance — 48 points, seven rebounds and 11 assists — from Trae Young. The Bucks could have been down, but they laughed it off and kept moving forward.

Before Antetokounmpo hyperextended his left knee in Game 4 of the Eastern Conference finals, the Bucks regularly posted videos of Tucker laughing with Antetokounmpo, the NBA's two-time MVP.

Before joining the Bucks, like most players around the league, Tucker knew very little about Antetokounmpo, but they have quickly developed a friendship.

"If you see all the videos, I'm always laughing because he is hilarious," Tucker said of the Bucks star. "You really don't know. He's really funny. He'll say anything. He's real. He's going to tell you some real stuff. He's going to keep it real with you. It'll catch you off guard because you wouldn't expect it, like the way he comes with it, the way he says stuff. You wouldn't expect it and I don't think anybody would that didn't really know him."

As the Bucks approached the Finals, Tucker did more than just fit with his new roster; he came to shape its identity. With an injury to Donte DiVincenzo against the Heat in the first round, Tucker took his place in the starting lineup against the Nets and then held onto that spot as the Bucks went up against the Hawks. When Antetokounmpo went down in Game 4, the Bucks decided to switch, a Tucker specialty, on defense for the entirety of the final two games against the Hawks.

"Toughness. He brings that mental physicality that you need to win in the league," Bobby Portis said during Monday's media availability. "All guys,

P.J. Tucker hits a 3-pointer over Atlanta Hawks forward Danilo Gallinari during the Game 4 of the Eastern Conference Finals in Atlanta.

all teams need a guy like him on your roster that do all the little things. It's just not about scoring with him, whether he's making shots or missing them. He's the same way every day. Brings that dog to the team, brings that toughness that every team needs, like I said, getting all the loose balls, fighting for the offensive rebounds, coming out of the corners and getting rebounds, things like that. Always gets a big rebound every game.

"He does all the little things for our basketball team that we really, really need, and he's great in his role. He plays it to a T."

Part of the reason Tucker initially felt underappreciated in Houston was the organization's unwillingness to negotiate an extension with him that he believed to reflect the value he brought to the Rockets. So with Tucker once again providing value and this time doing it with the Bucks on the way to the NBA Finals, the thing that might extend his happiness even longer could be guaranteeing a future in Milwaukee.

"No, no, I'm way past an extension now," Tucker said. "I'm free this summer. The last thing on my mind is an extension. I'm a free agent this summer, so I'll be able to make some decisions myself.

"I'm excited to be free. I'm really excited to be able to pick where I want to go, so I'm excited. The extension thing was for a different period of time. We didn't even talk about that when I came to Milwaukee. There was no extension. I just wanted to come play and get a chance to do what I do and that was it. I just wanted to have a chance."

In Milwaukee, Tucker received that chance and he has given himself an opportunity to prove it all one more time on the game's biggest stage. ═══

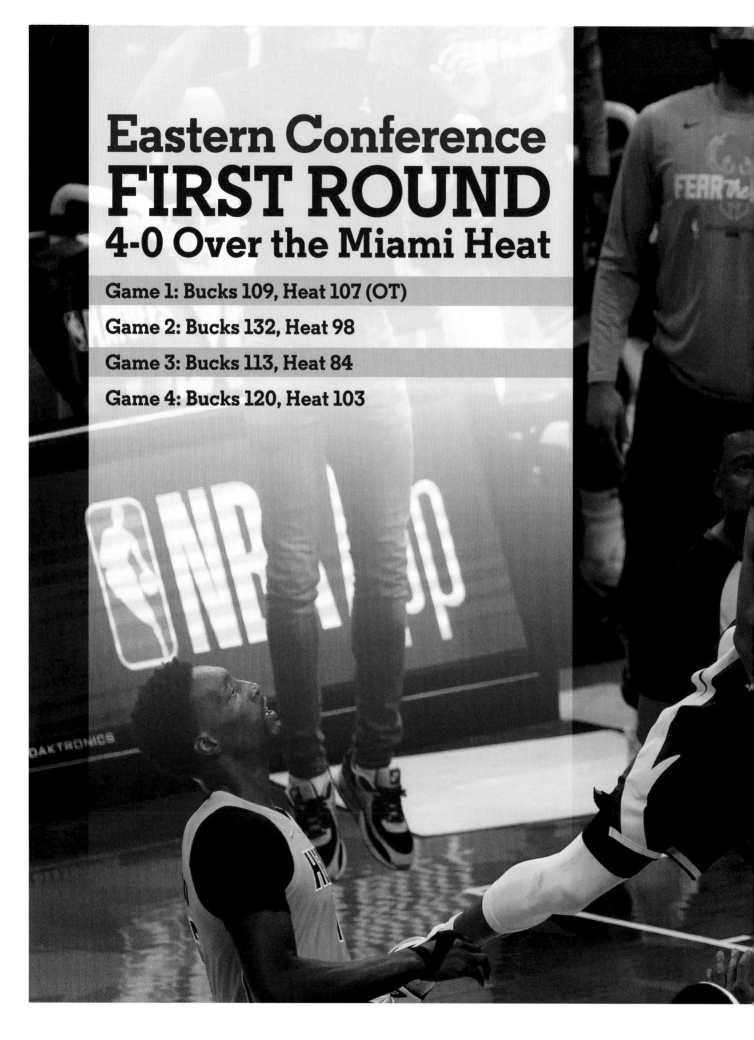

Eastern Conference
FIRST ROUND
4-0 Over the Miami Heat

Game 1: Bucks 109, Heat 107 (OT)

Game 2: Bucks 132, Heat 98

Game 3: Bucks 113, Heat 84

Game 4: Bucks 120, Heat 103

'That's What He Does'

Khris Middleton's Clutch Moments Have Become Familiar for Bucks

By Eric Nehm | May 22, 2021

Brook Lopez has grown tired of the question. During his three seasons in Milwaukee, the Bucks center has regularly watched Khris Middleton take — and make — big shots in clutch moments. Then, invariably after the game, reporters ask Lopez about his confidence in Middleton in those moments or Middleton's ability to rebound from missing a few shots in the fourth quarter and then step up in the game's biggest moment or Middleton's steely demeanor in pressure situations. Lopez has answered some version of the question so many times that he has joked that his answer is beginning to feel stale.

Nevertheless, Lopez laughed and smiled as he answered the question yet again Saturday after Middleton nailed a game-winning pull-up jumper with 0.5 seconds remaining in overtime to give the Bucks a 109-107 win in Game 1 of his team's first-round playoff series with the Miami Heat.

"You could look up a ton of other times I answered that question for you, and they would all be valid," Lopez said. "He's just always so level. Obviously, first game of the playoffs, everybody's amped up. Big game. This could have been a preseason game to him. I think he would have been the same way in the moment, shooting the ball and everything."

And the moment was anything but normal.

The Bucks had just given up a tying 3 to Goran Dragic, which came off a tipped-out offensive rebound of a 3-pointer Jimmy Butler airballed late in the shot clock. It's the type of play that could discombobulate any team, and yet, Middleton was ready for the moment. As head coach Mike Budenholzer let his team play without a timeout, Middleton calmly ran down the floor, got position on Duncan Robinson and popped out to receive the ball from Jrue Holiday near half court. From there, it was pretty simple.

Khris Middleton makes a basket over the Miami Heat's Duncan Robinson in the final seconds of overtime of Game 1, setting the tone for the first-round playoff series.

"Brook came up and set the screen," Holiday explained. "Trevor (Ariza) switched onto him. I think (Middleton) saw Trevor kind of jump out, and he took the lane to the right to kind of go back towards Duncan. Faded on him. Game."

"I just tried to give him a good screen and get him open," Lopez added. "And he made a fantastic play as usual."

"Just trying to get to a spot where I knew I could possibly get a shot up or hit Brook for a roll," Middleton said. "Ended up getting to the spot for a shot, just raise up and just shoot it, try to get the last one. Taking as much time off the clock as I can and live with the results afterwards."

Middleton has done this before. He hit a late 3 to seal the Bucks' lone win against the Heat in the second round last season, a score-tying baseline bucket to force overtime in Game 3 against the Raptors in the 2019 Eastern Conference finals and a 3-pointer with 0.5 seconds left to force overtime in the opening game of the Bucks' 2018 playoff series against the Celtics. And yet, this year's annual clutch-time postseason bucket felt like the most significant one to date.

Saturday's game was not pretty. Middleton led all scorers with 27 points (six rebounds and six assists), but he was just 10-of-22 from the field. Giannis Antetokounmpo trailed him by one point with 26 points (18 rebounds and six assists) but took 27 shots to get that total. The Bucks made just five of the 31 3-pointers they attempted. On the other side, Butler and Bam Adebayo scored 26 points total on a combined 8-of-37 shooting.

Both teams struggled to get anything going offensively. Part of that might have been the five-day layoff for both teams, but the game was hard-fought and physical. It was gritty and more than a little ugly, the type of game most would associate with the Heat, not the Bucks. But on Saturday, the Bucks won ugly, and they pulled out

the victory because Middleton stepped up in the biggest moment.

"He was able to get to his spot, rise up and, you know, that's what he does," Antetokounmpo said. "Having a guy like Khris with the ball down the stretch, you know what's going to come."

While Middleton made the big shot for the Bucks, they would not have been there without the effort of the other two members of their big three.

With 5:30 remaining in the fourth quarter, Antetokounmpo sustained a left elbow injury trying to fight through an Adebayo screen, but he kept playing. He actively tried to keep his left elbow from making contact with any other players, which was particularly difficult considering he needed to fight over the top of dribble handoffs and screens, but that didn't keep him from going as hard as possible.

On a play in the final minute of regulation, knowing there was a good chance Butler's full body weight might come down on his injured left arm, Antetokounmpo reached in and poked the ball away, and then went down to the ground to fight for the loose ball with Butler. Eventually, officials called a jump ball. Middleton won the jump ball by tipping it to Antetokounmpo, who was then fouled by the Heat with 9.0 seconds remaining. Antetokounmpo made just one of two at the line (6 of 13 for the game), and Butler blew past him for a finger roll on the next possession to force overtime.

While that could have been another situation where the Bucks felt dispirited, Antetokounmpo kept playing and got the Bucks' first basket of the overtime period through sheer effort.

"That effort was huge for us. Everybody knows it," Middleton said. "He didn't shoot the ball the way I think he wanted to, but he didn't give up on it. He still made those extra plays. Diving on the ball, getting rebounds, extra hustle plays to keep us in the ball game. That's what helped us win tonight."

The same things could be said of Holiday, who made two of the game's biggest plays in the final minute of overtime. The first was snatching up a long defensive rebound and turning it into a layup in four seconds to give the Bucks a three-point lead with 39.3 seconds left.

"I saw Donte (DiVincenzo) go hit Bam on the boxout, and Donte's always around the rim and always knows where the ball is coming, but I saw that he was going to miss short," Holiday said after his 20-point, 11-rebound performance. "And I kind of took the angle towards the free-throw line to get the ball, and from there, I just had a full head of steam and really just had to concentrate on the layup."

The play was all about instincts and effort, but there is a level of innate skill in the movement. Few players in the NBA could put all of that together and make that play in that moment, but Holiday did it. And then he did it again on the game's final play.

While Middleton tried to take the game's final shot to not give the Heat a chance to answer, his shot went through the rim with half a second remaining on the clock, which meant the Bucks needed to get one more stop. With such limited time, the Heat needed to find a way to get off a quick shot, so they ran Butler off a screen toward the near-side corner, and it was Holiday's job to seal the victory.

"Just staying in front. We don't want any 3s, I mean, we don't want 2s either, but I didn't want to get beat backdoor to the rim for a tip," Holiday said. "And then, if I saw the ball, there's 0.5 seconds left, so there was no way he could pump fake, so I went up with him and tried to block it."

The shot was reminiscent of the final shot Butler took to end Game 2 of last season's second-round series between the two teams.

In that game, Middleton drew a foul on a 3-point attempt and knocked down three clutch free throws to tie the score with 4.3 seconds remaining. The Heat turned to Butler for the last shot, and he isolated against Wesley Matthews before trying a fadeaway jumper from the left corner, just like he did on Saturday, but Antetokounmpo came over as a helper and was whistled for a foul. Butler calmly stepped to the free-throw line and hit both free throws with no time remaining to give the Heat a 2-0 series lead and the Bucks a whole lot to contemplate.

On Saturday, because of the grit and determination of the Bucks' big three, the roles from last season have been reversed. The Bucks won ugly and took the first game of the series, and the Heat are left to think about what could have been. ▬▬

Acing the Test

Bucks Avenge the Bubble, Sweep the Heat. So What Was Learned?

By Eric Nehm | May 29, 2021

As he put together back-to-back MVP seasons, Giannis Antetokounmpo was quite open about how he wanted to play on the offensive end of the floor. Following the Bucks' first deep postseason run in his first MVP season, Antetokounmpo candidly told *The Athletic* about how the strength he gained between his fifth and sixth seasons made him feel as though he could just "go and dunk it" on a lot of possessions.

Following a season-high 47 points against the Trail Blazers in April, Antetokounmpo joked that while he is always trying to work on his game, "if I can get into the paint 20 out of 20 times, I'll get into the paint 20 times." For Antetokounmpo, the preference is always getting to the basket and dominating the paint.

Reminded of some of his previous thoughts following his first career playoff triple-double (20 points, 12 rebounds, 15 assists) in the Bucks' 120-103 Game 4 first-round playoff victory against the Miami Heat on Saturday, Antetokounmpo wanted to first ask for a quick clarification on the thoughts he shared previously.

"When did I say that? Last year?" Antetokounmpo asked." There's no way I said it this year."

His immediate visceral reaction to a reminder of those previous thoughts was a strong indicator of just how much things have changed for the Bucks this season.

Before twisting his ankle in Game 4 and missing the conclusion of the Bucks' second-round 2020 playoff series against the Heat, Antetokounmpo tried to drive straight through the stout wall of defenders to keep him from the rim. He turned the ball over, picked up charges and took a physical beating. The Bucks' offense floundered and they lost the series.

On Saturday, Antetokounmpo had 13 assists before he scored a layup with 10 minutes, 42 seconds remaining in the fourth quarter for 10 points and the playoff triple-double, the franchise's first since Kareem Abdul-Jabbar (1970) and Paul Pressey (1986) accomplished the feat.

"There's growth in basketball," Antetokounmpo said. "I try to affect the game in any way I can and I'm blessed enough to — I can affect the game defensively, I can pass the ball. There are going to be days where I can be dominant and I'm mature enough to understand there's going to be days where I'm going to be able to do it and there are going to be days where I'm not going to be able to do it."

With 20 points, 12 rebounds and 15 assists in Game 4, Giannis Antetokounmpo notched his first ever playoff triple double as the Bucks completed their first-round sweep.

While the Bucks made significant personnel changes in the last year and the new players on the roster made a significant impact in the series, the playoff outcome against the Heat this season was different because of how the Bucks evolved as a team. They handle adversity better and seem to be cool and calm in pressure-packed situations and that was on full display in their Game 4 win.

In two consecutive postseasons, the Bucks did not have an answer for "the wall" teams built against Antetokounmpo. On Saturday, the Bucks made it look easy.

The Heat frustrated the Bucks in the first half by mixing in some zone defense and building the wall just like they did last season, which led them to a seven-point halftime lead. Rather than panic and try to break down the wall by running through it and picking up offensive fouls, Antetokounmpo remained patient and found his teammates as the Bucks made their comeback in the third quarter.

"Miami is a great team, very disciplined team," Antetokounmpo said. "They're always going to be there. They don't relax. There's not a play that there is going to be a wall and then the second play, there is not going to be a wall. They're going to be there for 48 minutes.

"That's what makes Miami a great defensive team and that's what makes them great, but at the end of the day, guys were right there. Bobby (Portis) was wide open. Bryn (Forbes) was wide open. Pat (Connaughton) was wide open. Khris (Middleton) was wide open at times and I think that's the maturity of being able to affect the game in multiple ways and not just go and get in the paint and dunk it."

Those shooters were open because of the new offense installed at the start of the season, which put a man in "the dunker" spot at all times and lengthened the distance between Antetokounmpo and open shooters.

"Don't get me wrong, if I can dunk it every single play, I'll dunk it every single play," Antetokounmpo said. "But just being mature and having my head up and looking for guys when they're open, it was big for us tonight. It was big for us the whole series. I tried to do that last year also, but man, this year, guys were knocking down shots.

"It was beautiful to watch. BP (Bobby Portis) was fucking amazing. Bryn was amazing. Jrue (Holiday) was amazing. Khris was amazing. Whoever I threw the ball, they were just making everything. PJ was amazing. And Brook (Lopez) just being a presence down there. Once they built the wall, there was a tower behind the wall named Brook that was wide-open every single time. He was just so big in the paint, so dominant in the paint and we were able to try to punish them every single possession."

The Bucks' growth and maturity were not just limited to what they did offensively either.

One year after failing to keep up with the seemingly endless cutting of the Heat offense and finding no answers to slow down Jimmy Butler and Goran Dragic, the Bucks shut down the Heat.

For the series, Butler averaged 14.5 points, 7.5 rebounds and 7.0 assists per game and made just 29.7 percent of his shots, one year after averaging 23.4 points, 5.8 rebounds, and 4.4 assists per game on 53.2 percent shooting against the Bucks.

Similarly, after putting up 17.2 points (60 percent shooting), 12.0 rebounds and 4.4 assists per game against the Bucks in the second round last season, Bam Adebayo averaged just 15.5 points per game on 46.4 percent shooting, as well as 9.3 rebounds and 4.3 assists per game.

Tactically, the major change was moving Antetokounmpo to Butler, which kept the Heat star from using his physicality to get where he wanted on the floor and making plays. But to Lopez, the Bucks defended the Heat better this

Khris Middleton shoots over the Miami Heat's Bam Adebayo, en route to 20 points on the night.

season because of an improved mindset.

"Aside from all X's and O's, I just thought our mentality was so great this year," Lopez said after a 25-point, 12-rebound performance on Saturday. "We came in with our game plan and everything like that, but above all, we wanted to outwork and outphysical them, have greater energy. And you know, again, Something else coach wrote on the board before every game, 'Don't expect anything, don't beg, just go out there, leave it on the floor.'

"It's our team, the five of us on the floor, the 11 other players, the coaching staff, we're all we have and regardless of what the refs do, the other team does, we gotta go out there and be ourselves each and every night."

With that mindset, the Bucks managed to discombobulate Miami, even when the Heat had an advantage.

All series long, the Heat saw Lopez or Antetokounmpo waiting for them at the rim and couldn't figure out how to beat it, which led to some frustration from the Heat and even a few moments where they lost their cool.

As Game 2 unraveled for the Heat, they started to foul Antetokounmpo to try to frustrate him. Ariza wrapped up Antetokounmpo on a layup and pushed off of Antetokounmpo to get back up after both had collapsed to the ground and Nemanja Bjelica took Antetokounmpo to the ground on another foul in the fourth quarter. Antetokounmpo never reacted and rolled his eyes at both attempts to rile him up. The same thing occurred in the fourth quarter of Game 4 as Dragic and Middleton got tangled up fighting for a rebound.

Following the game, Middleton (20 points, 11 rebounds) called it a dirty play, but also explained that he knew what Dragic was trying to do.

"I just know some things are more important than a personal battle," Middleton said. "So, just don't worry about it, laugh it off and continue to worry about the game."

In the end, Middleton stayed focused and the Bucks took care of business in the fourth quarter, outscoring the Heat by 11 in the period.

One season after feeling helpless as they struggled to figure out how to score against the Heat and couldn't consistently get defensive stops, the Bucks throttled the Heat in Game 4 and eliminated them from the postseason. The Heat are not the team they were last season, but they did present the best possible first-round test of everything the Bucks have been working on during the regular season.

And the Bucks aced it.

"Despite wins and losses in the regular season, whatever the end result was on one particular night, we definitely felt we got better and learned a lot throughout the regular season," Lopez said. "We had a lot of new bodies, a new offense to really get used to, so there were a lot of adjustments to be made and we knew all of that was for this time. Peaking at the right moment, we really feel like we're doing that and we still feel like we're getting better and improving each and every single night."

After the game, the Bucks could have dwelled on the redemption of beating the team that beat them in the playoffs last season after the game, but they didn't spend much time savoring the victory. Instead, they started to think about what comes next.

"We got a long way to go," Bucks coach Mike Budenholzer said. "It's the first round of the playoffs. And I think there's gotta be a humility, a humbleness, an attitude or a mindset to get better. We've advanced in the first round. Whoever we play next, we got to have a similar focus, a similar edge, willingness to play with each other, play together, all the things that we just did. It means nothing if we don't keep doing it going forward." ▬▬▬

Bryn Forbes improved on his stellar Game 2 performance, scoring 22 points on 7-of-14 shooting from 3-point range in Game 4.

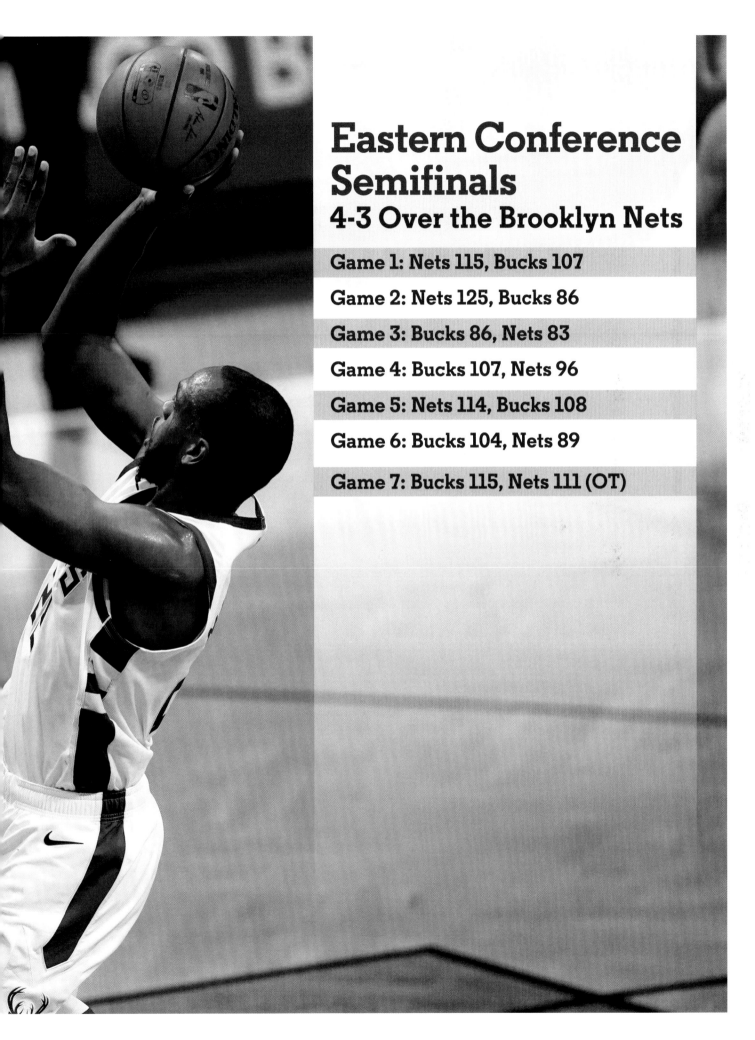

Eastern Conference Semifinals
4-3 Over the Brooklyn Nets

Game 1: Nets 115, Bucks 107

Game 2: Nets 125, Bucks 86

Game 3: Bucks 86, Nets 83

Game 4: Bucks 107, Nets 96

Game 5: Nets 114, Bucks 108

Game 6: Bucks 104, Nets 89

Game 7: Bucks 115, Nets 111 (OT)

How They Jrue It Up

Jrue Holiday's Mad Dash Helps Bucks Pull Out an Ugly,
Desperate and Much-Needed Game 3 Win

By Eric Nehm | June 11, 2021

Three feet separated Jrue Holiday from Kyrie Irving as the Nets guard brought the ball across the half-court line with 30 seconds remaining in Game 3 on Thursday night. With the Bucks trailing by a point and 12 seconds separating the game clock and shot clock, Holiday crouched down low in his defensive stance as he prepared for the possession that could decide the game and the Bucks' entire season.

As Holiday and Irving stood eye-to-eye, Bruce Brown made his way toward the pair, closely followed by Brook Lopez. Brown, the Nets' guard-turned-center, had served as one of the driving forces behind the Bucks' lead quickly shrinking in the first quarter by running this exact action. Again and again, the 6-foot-4 Brown sprinted up to set a screen for Irving or Kevin Durant and rained down floaters over the top of Lopez, as Irving and Durant found pockets of space to pass him the ball.

And that is exactly what unfolded as Irving turned the corner on his drive.

With Lopez backpedaling in front of Irving at the 3-point line, the Nets' point guard delivered a pocket pass to Brown. Lopez tried to get back in front of Brown, but Brown jump-stopped just inside the free throw line and tossed a floater high above Lopez's outstretched right arm. The ball made it over the top of the Bucks' big man, but fell short and bounced off the front of the rim to Giannis Antetokounmpo, who secured the rebound in traffic and dished it out to Holiday on the right sideline.

To this point, Holiday had made just three of the 13 shots he had attempted in 45 minutes on the floor, but with Bucks coach Mike Budenholzer urging him up the floor, Holiday brought the ball across halfcourt and hesitated slightly near Nets coach Steve Nash.

Jrue Holiday's clutch playmaking late in Game 3 helped the Bucks grind out their first win of the series against the Nets.

"At that point, I felt like maybe they thought I was gonna call a timeout," Holiday said. "I think in my head, I was kind of thinking, 'Well, maybe I should run some clock.' But I saw me and Bruce Brown one-on-one. So, I just made a move, and it was a good one and ended up getting a layup."

Holiday's spin move and finish might have caught the Nets' defenders by surprise, but not anyone with the Bucks.

"He's just that kind of guy," Budenholzer said. "To take the ball and get to the basket and finish with a scramble defense, we needed that. We needed that one play from him, and he made it. And it was big."

Despite the big play, which led to an 86-83 Game 3 win, the Bucks' work was far from over. With a one-point lead and 11.4 seconds remaining, the Bucks needed to get another stop on the Nets' sideline out-of-bounds play to secure a victory. The Nets tried to free up Durant with a screen from Joe Harris, but P.J. Tucker bodied him away from it, and Lopez helped as Tucker caught up.

Blake Griffin tried to find Brown after Lopez left him, but the ball flew past Brown and all the way from the left side of the floor to the right. Irving managed to chase it down and pitched it to Brown, as he fell out of bounds. Once again, Brown found himself in space with a lane to the basket and Lopez the only player around to contest the shot.

"Once I saw him get the ball, I just knew I had to try to meet him at the basket as best as possible," Lopez said. "He definitely had a head of steam and was going downhill, so I just tried to make the shot as difficult as possible."

The Bucks secured the rebound after the Brown miss, but they still had even more work to do. Khris Middleton needed to step to the line and make two free throws, which he did.

And the Bucks needed to get another stop. With 2.1 seconds left, the Nets had another sideline out-of-bounds play, and they again looked for Durant. This time, the Nets' wing received the inbounds pass and took one dribble before firing up a one-legged, 28-foot runner floating away from the basket. Durant's attempt missed off the back rim, and the Bucks picked up their first win of the series.

There was nothing pretty about the victory, but the Bucks didn't seem to mind.

"If we gotta muck up the game, then we gotta muck it up," Holiday said.

"A win is a win," Antetokounmpo said. "As I said last game, lose by 40, lose by one, it's still the same thing, we still lost. And (Thursday), we didn't score a lot. It didn't look as pretty, but at the end of the day, we got a win, and that's why we came and showed up tonight."

The Bucks escaped with a victory in Game 3 because of the hard-nosed defense (and Holiday's transition bucket) in the final 30 seconds, but the Bucks would not have been in a position to steal that game without the clutch shot-making of Middleton.

With 3:10 remaining, Nash called a timeout. Neither the Bucks nor the Nets had scored since a Durant jumper tied the score at 76 with 6:09 remaining. For three long minutes, both teams struggled immensely on the offensive end, but then Middleton and Durant broke their respective teams out of the game's collective funk. Coming out of the timeout, the Bucks gave Middleton the ball in pick-and-rolls in the middle of the floor and let him go to work. He traded jumpers on four consecutive possessions with Durant to tie the game at 80 before he missed a jumper and Durant made a 3 to give the Nets a three-point lead. After a timeout, Middleton got another basket on a Griffin goaltend and put the Bucks right back into the game.

By the end of the game, Middleton led all scorers with 35 points (12-of-25 shooting) to go along with 15 rebounds and also scored eight of the Bucks' final 10 points to pull out the victory in the final three minutes of the game.

"I just tried to make the right reads and make those shots," Middleton said. "I can see what they were trying to give me, just to try to take advantage of that. I feel like I can score in a lot of different ways. Those are the type of shots they want me to take, and I'm confident. I think I'm good enough. I worked on those shots a lot to knock them down, and they went down for me tonight."

While Middleton was great, the Bucks might not have been able to grab their first win in the series without Tucker's defense on Durant. While it can always be argued that an offensive player missed shots, Tucker made Durant work for everything in Game 3 during his 33 minutes on the floor. It could have just been an off-shooting night for Durant, who hit just 11-of-28 from the field, but Tucker draped himself on Durant all night, including a third-quarter fracas where the two players got in each other's faces and each received technical fouls.

"They played more physical," Durant said. "I think we got great looks. We didn't knock them down, but they also did a job of contesting and being physical and blocking shots at the rim."

And finally, the Bucks could not have pulled out a victory without the tone Antetokounmpo set in the first quarter. After a passive Game 2, Antetokounmpo (33 points, 14 rebounds) attacked the rim with force in the first quarter. On the way to 15 first-quarter points and a Bucks' 30-11 lead, Antetokounmpo threw down three dunks including a monstrous throwdown a minute into the game, which seemingly announced his intentions.

Each small piece enabled the Bucks to pull out a victory and protect their home court in the first game of the series at Fiserv Forum, but there may be trouble ahead.

Middleton and Antetokounmpo combined for 68 of the Bucks' 86 points on Thursday. It is great that both found success in Game 3, and it is possible the Middleton-Antetokounmpo pick-and-roll combination will unlock the Bucks' offense going forward, but the Bucks still scored just 86 points in Game 3, which brings their per-game series average to 93 points per game. For the third straight game, the Bucks' offense looked lost as they relied far too often on isolation play to create for their teammates.

Despite knowing the Nets would be switching everything, the Bucks still struggled to regularly create high-quality looks. Outside of Antetokounmpo and Middleton, the Bucks scored just 18 points on 8-of-34 shooting, including a 4-of-14 night for Holiday. The Bucks won, but they do not appear any closer to figuring out the Nets' switching defense.

On the other end, the Bucks held Durant to 30 points on 28 shots, but Durant never really looked uncomfortable. Durant still managed to hit a pull-up 3 to give the Nets an 83-80 lead in the final two minutes of the game and get enough space to fire a game-tying 3-pointer at the buzzer. He didn't shoot well, but he never appeared flustered, and there is a good chance he shoots at a much higher clip in Game 4. Also, Brown still appeared able to find weak spots in the Bucks' defense as the Nets' short roll extraordinaire.

As Antetokounmpo said, a win is a win and the Bucks do not have to apologize for winning an ugly game, but they still need to improve quite a few things on each side of the ball to feel comfortable about potentially making a comeback in this series. ▰▰▰

Get at Me Dog

P.J. Tucker has Nets Riled with Guarding of Kevin Durant as Bucks Draw Even in Series

By Eric Nehm | June 14, 2021

As Nets forward Blake Griffin inbounded the ball following a Khris Middleton bucket midway through the first quarter, Kevin Durant collected the pass and looked upcourt. Bucks forward P.J. Tucker stood waiting for him before the half-court line.

Tucker did not retreat as Durant brought the ball up the floor but instead got into a defensive stance. When Durant saw that, he picked up his pace and broke into a jog up the floor. Tucker responded in kind and started to backpedal, but when he reached the half-court line some 10 feet in front of Durant, he swiveled his hips to avoid an oncoming screen from Bruce Brown. After managing to avoid the screen, Tucker recovered back to Durant, who was now dribbling on the right wing near the 3-point line. As Tucker approached, Durant used his left hand to shield Tucker from getting to the ball but ultimately kicked the ball back out to Brown when he saw Bobby Portis enter the fray from the backside off the defense.

Typically, this might grant Durant a momentary reprieve, but not with Tucker defending him. The pass gave Tucker, the tenacious 6-foot-5 forward, a chance to root himself underneath Durant's lanky frame and to body Durant to keep him from getting the ball again.

From 5 feet away, Brown lofted the ball up over the top of Tucker to Durant in the right corner of the floor. Durant caught the ball and planted his left foot. He opened up towards the basket and tried to use his right leg and right shoulder to take the space Tucker occupied, but Tucker held his ground. Durant ripped the ball through low and drove the baseline. Tucker remained connected to Durant, who planted and jumped off 2 feet through Tucker and toward the rim. On his way up, Tucker and Portis combined to block his shot.

As the Nets and Bucks fought for the loose ball, Durant turned to official Tony Brothers in disbelief, unable to comprehend how no foul had been called on Tucker.

P.J. Tucker provided the spark the Bucks needed in Game 4, scoring 13 points while aggressively defending Kevin Durant. (USA Today Sports)

It was just the start of Durant's day against Tucker, which ended with Durant scoring 28 points but making only nine of the 25 shots he attempted in the Bucks' 107-96 Game 4 victory. All night, Durant complained to officials about what he deemed to be excessive contact from Tucker, and Nets coach Steve Nash followed suit after the game.

"He's playing extremely physical and made it difficult," Nash said. "That's his role on their team, and I thought it was borderline non-basketball physical at times, but that's the playoffs. You have to adapt and adjust."

Unsurprisingly, Bucks coach Mike Budenholzer had a different opinion.

"He's just guarding him," Budenholzer said. "If that's not basketball, I don't know what is. We just gotta keep the same mindset to guard (Durant), to make everything tough, so nothing changes. P.J. is a very good individual defender. Puts a lot of time in studying film work, understanding tendencies and those things. It's just guarding."

While Tucker was not putting any points on the scoreboard with his defense on Durant, he was helping prevent Durant from scoring and, more importantly, setting the tone for the Bucks in a game they needed to win. With each reach and each bump and each stop, Tucker provided the example his teammates needed to follow and the energy the Bucks needed to survive a strong start from the Nets.

"I think it's contagious," Pat Connaughton said. "It's something that we need. And obviously, there's times that we need it more, there's times that we need it less, depending how the game is being called from an officiating standpoint, but we need the intensity there all the time. The physicality, you can turn it up sometimes, you can turn it down sometimes, but the intensity has to be there at all times and it's contagious."

With Tucker providing the spark, the Bucks responded when the Nets hit them hardest. After the Nets put together an 8-0 run to take a 34-23 lead at the beginning of the second quarter without Durant on the floor, the Bucks turned to a little-used small-ball unit with Jrue Holiday, Connaughton, Middleton, Giannis Antetokounmpo and Tucker on the floor once Durant returned. And that group ripped off a 14-2 run to retake a 37-36 lead, but in a strange role reverse, Tucker provided the offense, while his teammates did the little things and still followed his lead on defense.

After a couple of switches on the defensive end forced a missed 3-pointer by Mike James, it was Antetokounmpo who ran a perfect lane down the middle of the floor to draw the attention of Durant and open up Tucker for a corner 3 and Middleton hit him on time and on target with the perfect pass.

Then, Tucker fought around a Nic Claxton screen and drew an offensive foul.

And then Connaughton and Antetokounmpo fought for an offensive rebound before Connaughton chased it down and found Tucker in the corner for a 3-pointer.

Antetokounmpo led the Bucks in scoring with 34 points (and 12 rebounds). Middleton added 19 points and eight assists, and Holiday found his footing offensively with 14 points and nine assists, but Tucker was the player who led the Bucks to a Game 4 win to even the series on Sunday. He was the one who fueled the team's second-quarter answer to the Nets' big run and the defensive tenacity the Bucks needed to take Game 4 and even the series.

And Tucker will be the one who has to do it again Tuesday.

Late in the second quarter, Nets guard Kyrie Irving injured his right ankle and missed the remainder of Game 4. Nash said X-rays on Irving's ankle were negative following the game, but a source told The Athletic's Alex Schiffer that Irving left the building in a walking boot on his right foot and used crutches as he walked to the team bus to make his way back to Brooklyn. Before the game, Nash told reporters the team's other superstar, James Harden, was progressing

Giannis Antetokounmpo and P.J. Tucker celebrate after a third-quarter basket against the Nets. (USA Today Sports)

in rehabbing his hamstring injury but did not provide a concrete timeline on when Harden might return to game action. As of now, it appears as though Durant will be the lone member of the Nets' big three on the floor, which means Tucker's ability to bother Durant once again will be paramount to the Bucks' success.

"I think P.J. just has to keep thinking, 'How can we do it?' going into the next game and just keep that mindset of just competing and contesting and making everything hard," Budenholzer said. "P.J. is a veteran, navigating a lot of screens. He's getting hit a lot, but his physical toughness, his mental toughness — he's just gotta keep coming and contest and make everything hard on Durant."

And his teammates will have to follow his lead. With two members of the Nets' big three likely out for Game 5 on Tuesday, the Bucks will have a chance to steal the road victory they need to win this second-round series, something they failed to do twice at the start of the series, and advance to the Eastern Conference Finals.

"When we went to Brooklyn last (week), in my opinion, we got embarrassed," Connaughton said. "It was something that we needed to take a little more ownership in and a little more pride in and understanding that, 'Hey, we need to be better. And we need to find a way to try to get a win on the road.' We are the lower seed. We are the team that is going to have to go on the road, at least one more time, maybe two, we got to find a way to win a road game. And we got to bring that tenacity, that toughness and have each other's backs in a hostile environment."

After the Bucks held the Miami Heat to 84 points on May 27 to secure the Bucks' first road win of the postseason and a 3-0 series lead, it was Tucker who claimed their roster was full of "dogs" this season and ready to prove outsider perceptions of the team wrong. In Game 5, the Bucks will have that chance on the road in Brooklyn, and it can all start with Tucker's underdog mentality. ▬▬▬

Taking the Challenge

I Asked Giannis About Guarding Kevin Durant.
'Let's Have a Conversation.' So We Did.

By Eric Nehm | June 16, 2021

After dropping the first two games of their second-round playoff series to the Nets, the Bucks went back to Milwaukee to try to figure out how to slow down Kevin Durant and the Nets. With heavy doses of physicality and savvy from veteran wing P.J. Tucker, as well as injuries to Durant's co-stars James Harden and Kyrie Irving, the Bucks appeared to have found the answers. After watching Durant torch them for 30.5 points per game on 55.8 percent shooting in Brooklyn, the Bucks held Durant to 58 total points on 37.7 percent shooting and took both games at Fiserv Forum in Milwaukee to even the series.

With a chance to set up an opportunity to close out the Nets at home, the Bucks watched Durant do something no other player has ever done. Durant became the first player in NBA history to tally at least 45 points, 15 rebounds and 10 assists in a playoff game with 49, 17 and 10 in the Nets' 114-108 victory Tuesday for a 3-2 series lead.

The historic performance left the Bucks lost and once again searching for answers to questions they just can't seem to solve when it comes to Durant's prodigious offensive talent. Bucks star Giannis Antetokounmpo (34 points, 12 rebounds, four assists) found himself so desperate for an answer that he flipped the question around on The Athletic when asked what he believed the Bucks could have done differently to make it tougher on Durant.

"What do you think?" Antetokounmpo asked. "Let's have a conversation."

It was hard to blame the Bucks star for feeling that way. Durant had just put on one of the most amazing playoff performances of all time. In one of the game's biggest moments, Khris Middleton denied Durant the ball for the first 21 seconds of a Nets possession before

Khris Middleton and the Bucks couldn't do much to slow down a scorching hot Kevin Durant in Game 5 and found themselves with their backs against the wall again heading into Game 6 at home in Milwaukee.

the lanky forward caught the ball near the half-court line, took one dribble and rose up for a deep off-balance 3 that went straight through the net to give the Nets a four-point lead.

There is simply not much for a defense to do to stop that type of shotmaking.

"He hit some extremely tough shots," Middleton said following a 25-point, five-assist performance in the Game 5 loss. "That's what he's been doing his whole career. He's one of the best scorers. We definitely saw it up-close and personal tonight."

While Durant ended the game with a monster stat line, he actually had a relatively modest first quarter with just seven points. Despite not scoring all that much, Durant managed to create serious foul trouble for the Bucks, which point guard Jrue Holiday believed played a major role in allowing Durant to eventually have the big night.

"I had three fouls in the first half," Holiday said after the loss. "Tuck had two. Giannis had two. I feel like a lot of those aren't equal or the same on both sides of the ball."

The Bucks ran out to an early double-digit lead, but the second quarter turned into a rough patch for the Bucks as coach Mike Budenholzer attempted to balance a rotation full of players he deemed to be in serious early foul trouble. Instead of using the team's normal rotations, Budenholzer shuffled in reserve guards Elijah Bryant and Pat Connaughton for longer-than-normal stints in unusual lineups to get his regulars into the second half with a more reasonable number of fouls, and it helped keep the Nets within striking distance, 59-43, at the half.

Middleton disagreed with his teammate's assessment during his postgame news conference. While Holiday believed it was the Bucks' early foul trouble that fueled Durant's impressive night. Middleton seemed to think it was the start of the second half when Durant made finding his teammates a priority. Rather than free himself up by making shots, Durant created the attention and started to get his teammates open shots.

"KD did a great job first distributing," Middleton said. "Blake and Jeff Green, they got hot from 3. That's what got them going, and then KD followed them right after that on one of his runs."

In the third quarter, Durant recorded five assists before unleashing his full scoring arsenal on the Bucks.

While Tucker kept Durant from getting comfortable on drives when the Nets visited Milwaukee for Games 3 and 4, Durant regularly turned the corner against Tucker on Tuesday night. With the Bucks once again trying to apply full-court pressure to varying degrees, Nets head coach Steve Nash changed the Nets' screening angles and took advantage of Tucker's aggressiveness. Instead of setting screens for Durant near the 3-point line, the Nets often put their screeners on the midcourt logo and let Durant start his pick-and-roll possessions much farther away from the basket.

The effect of moving those screens up the floor was two-fold. First, it created the space Durant needed to turn the corner and still attempt a pull-up 3-pointer, if that was what the play warranted. Second, it created a much larger space for Durant to attack Bucks center Brook Lopez off the dribble. With a more compressed space to attack in Games 3 and 4, Durant never had a chance to take advantage of his quickness against both Tucker and Lopez. The cluttered half-court space did not allow Durant to regularly rise up for clean looks or fully exploit his quickness and length to get past Lopez and finish at the rim.

When the Bucks decided to take Lopez off the floor and go with a switchy, small-ball unit early in the fourth quarter, Durant just found the weakest link on the defense and attacked it.

By the end of the game, Durant was scoring on all three levels and, much to Holiday's chagrin, also getting to the free-throw line. He scored 31 second-half points and took Game 5 from the Bucks, while his main running mate Harden remained mostly stationary in his first game back since reinjuring his hamstring in the first 30 seconds of Game 1. While Harden's name will show up in the box score for five points and eight assists, Durant was the one doing it all for the Nets.

So, back to the conversation with Antetokounmpo. How could the Bucks have done better against the Nets in Game 5, and how do they improve for Game 6?

"Just keep making it tough. Obviously, one of the best scorers to ever play the game," Antetokounmpo said. "It's tough. He's the best player in the world right now, and we've got to beat him as a team. We've got to guard him as a team, and we've got to make him make tough shots, like tonight, and we've just got to keep doing our job, and hopefully, he's going to miss. But we've got to keep doing our job, keep guarding together, keep showing help, keep making it tough, keep picking him up full court.

"We have to just keep containing him as much as possible, but at the end of the day, he's done an unbelievable job. Best player in the world, best scorer in the world. ... There's going to be nights where he's going to do what he did tonight and have 50, and there's going to be nights that we're going to try to contain him as much as possible and give ourselves a chance to be in the game and be in position to win the game."

When the idea of doubling Durant to force him to pass and make someone else create came up after the game, Budenholzer told reporters, "you think of everything," but the Bucks never opted to do that Tuesday night. They also opted against using Antetokounmpo as Durant's primary defender for a meaningful amount of time, but if Antetokounmpo has his way, that will change in Game 6.

"I want to take the challenge, and obviously everybody's gonna have a chance to guard him, but I would love going into Game 6 to be able to guard him and if coach want me to do that, I'm ready for that," Antetokounmpo said.

When the idea of doubling Durant to force the ball out of his hands and make someone else create

came up after the game, Budenholzer suggested the Bucks had thought through that idea but decided against implementing it.

"You think of everything," Budenholzer said. "You kind of go through it. You see how the series has evolved and a special performance by him. Credit to him, some tough shots. So, we got to look at it figure out getting better, but special by him."

The Bucks also opted against using Antetokounmpo as Durant's primary defender for a meaningful amount of time in Game 5. Budenholzer experimented with using Antetokounmpo as the primary defender more this season, including on Durant in the regular season and against Jimmy Butler in the first round, but did not use that option on Tuesday. If Antetokounmpo has his way, that will change in Game 6.

"I want to take the challenge, and obviously, everybody's gonna have a chance to guard him, but I would love going into Game 6 to be able to guard him and if coach wants me to do that, I'm ready for that," Antetokounmpo said.

If the Bucks plan on stopping Durant in Game 6 and forcing a Game 7, they will need to have a real conversation as a team about how to get it done. And they cannot only think through everything; they will have to be willing to try everything in order to save their season. ▬▬

Khash Money

Khris Middleton 'Did a Little Bit of Everything' to Force Bucks-Nets Game 7

By Eric Nehm | June 18, 2021

The whistle blew and Nets guard James Harden immediately made his way toward official Kane Fitzgerald.

Harden pointed towards the floor with his right hand and then started gesturing to show exactly what had happened on the play. As the league's preeminent 3-point foul-drawing practitioner, Harden could explain exactly what actually occurred on the play as opposed to what the official believed he saw go down. So, Harden started to describe it as Fitzgerald walked toward the scorer's table to signal a foul on Joe Harris and give three free throws to Khris Middleton with 8:20 left in Thursday's Game 6, an elimination game for the Bucks.

With the three-shot foul still being called, Harden peeled off of Fitzgerald and moved to Nets coach Steve Nash to instruct him to call a timeout and challenge the play. By the time Nash called that timeout, Middleton had the ball in his hands at the free-throw line, but the Nets were granted the timeout anyway. In the end, though, they decided against challenging the play. The fiction Harden was selling seemed better for the Nets than the reality in front of them: Middleton had gotten the Nets one last time.

The Bucks put together a wire-to-wire 104-89 victory in Game 6 over the Nets on Thursday, but that doesn't mean the Nets just let the Bucks run away with an easy win to force a Game 7 on Saturday in Brooklyn. The Nets continued to play hard and chipped away at the Bucks' lead throughout the game, but just couldn't get over the hump. In fact, the final three times the Nets chopped the Bucks' lead down to five, Middleton — 38 points (on 16 shots), 10 rebounds, five assists, five steals — was there to answer and push the Nets back once again.

"He had a great game with timely possessions," Jrue Holiday (21 points, eight rebounds and five assists) said following the win. "He really carried us through those moments when we needed a lift. He's done it all year and you know it's win or go home, and he took it upon himself to go ahead and do that."

Khris Middleton had his way with the Nets in a comfortable Game 6 win, dropping 38 points on only 16 shots, and adding 10 rebounds, five assists and five steals.

Harris clearly fouled Middleton on the play. He put his left hand on Middleton's right arm multiple times during the possession and Middleton simply took a 3-point shot while Harris was doing it. The play leading up to the foul, however, showed just how much the Bucks trust Middleton and the level at which he executed on Thursday night.

With 10 seconds left on the shot clock at the start of the inbounds play, it looked like Giannis Antetokounmpo might be coming up to set a screen for a late pick-and-roll, but eventually, Middleton just made something for himself. As The Athletic's analytics expert Seth Partnow has pointed out throughout the series, the Bucks have relied far too much on isolation and self-created shots. But in Game 6, Middleton was in such great offensive rhythm that the Bucks could get away with it.

"Khris was amazing," Bucks forward P.J. Tucker said. "When Khris gets it going, I mean, we've all seen it, he makes it real easy on everybody because people have to help and they have to respect him."

At the end of the third quarter, the Nets cut the Bucks' lead to five, 72-67, with 1:27 remaining in the period and once again, Middleton was ready to take over.

It started with the mid-range jumper off of an offensive rebound from Tucker, but continued on the next play.

After the Bucks got a stop on a tough, contested Harden 3-pointer, Middleton caught the ball on the left wing in semi-transition and blew by Harris for a mid-range jumper. Then, after Durant went a little too early and missed a floater with six seconds left in the third quarter, Middleton snagged the rebound and tossed an outlet pass to Antetokounmpo underneath the basket to beat the buzzer. However, Antetokounmpo got too far under the basket and just needed to throw something up, Middleton, of course, was there and cleaned up the offensive rebound with a quick lay-up to beat the buzzer and to complete a personal 6-0 run to give the Bucks an 11-point lead heading into the final period.

"He loves those moments," Antetokounmpo said. "He's never scared of those moments. It's been an amazing eight years now having him next to me because I know in games like this he's always ready. He's always going to give his best, everything he has."

And while Middleton helped keep the door shut on a Nets' comeback multiple times in the second half, he was also the one that opened up the Bucks' double-digit halftime lead with 17 second-quarter points, including 3-pointers on back-to-back possessions near the end of the half.

"He did a little bit of everything," Bucks coach Mike Budenholzer said. "He came up with timely 3s. I thought the ball movement to get him some good looks, got him a little bit of a rhythm in that second quarter off of some penetration and kicks. I think a big offensive rebound by P.J. Tucker and kick out. He gets fouled on a 3-pointer when it got down to five. He just scored in a lot of different ways. That's what we need."

While Middleton played the starring role in Game 6, he was not alone in sending the series back to Brooklyn. Seemingly each time Middleton made a few shots to give the Bucks some breathing room, Antetokounmpo (30 points, 17 rebounds) was right behind him to push the lead out even further by attacking in transition and getting to the rim. Tucker hounded Kevin Durant for 34 minutes on defense and managed to keep multiple Bucks' possessions alive with three offensive rebounds and a few others he forced the Nets to tip out of bounds. Brook Lopez got back in the paint and hit the offensive glass for the first time since the start of the series. And despite a poor shooting night, Holiday still managed to contribute across the board with 21 points, 10 rebounds, five assists and four steals.

Pulling out a win felt good on Thursday night, but it will mean little if the Bucks do not also manage to pull out a Game 7 victory in Brooklyn on Saturday. Thus far in the series, the home team has won every game, so why should anyone believe

Kevin Durant had another nice scoring outing in Game 6 with 32 points, but Giannis Antetokounmpo and the Bucks made it harder on him this time around, as Durant took 30 shots in the process.

the Bucks can be the ones to reverse the trend?

"Since Game 3 until Game 6, we played four great games, four great games. And we just got to keep doing it. Keep trusting one another. Keep trusting our habits. Keep making it tough for them. Unfortunately. Game 5 didn't go our way, but it was a good game. We pushed them to their limits."

While the Bucks have played nowhere near their best basketball in this series, Antetokounmpo does have a point about the last four games of the series. Excluding their second-half collapse in Game 5, the Bucks have outplayed the Nets for four straight games. It hasn't been pretty, but it is hard

to argue. The Bucks have scored just 104.7 points per 100 possession in those four games, but they have only allowed 98.2 points per 100 possessions for a plus-6.5 net rating. Whether because of the Nets' injuries or the Bucks' improved play, the Bucks have been the better team for the last week.

"As I've said all season long, we are built for this moment, simple as that," Antetokounmpo said. "And nobody said it's going to be easy. It might be hard, but we are capable of doing it."

Now the Bucks just have to prove it with both teams' seasons hanging in the balance in Game 7. ▬▬

The Marathon Continues

Bucks Prevail in Epic Game 7, Advance to Eastern Conference Finals

By Eric Nehm | June 20, 2021

As Kevin Durant's shot at the end of overtime hung in the air, Jrue Holiday had a bad feeling.

"As I see the ball as I turn around, it's right on line," Holiday said. "So that's scary."

It was tough to blame him for feeling impending doom with that ball dropping towards the rim. Durant had already scored 48 points on the night and five minutes earlier, he had hit nearly the exact same shot over Bucks forward P.J. Tucker to force overtime. This time, however, it was well short. The Bucks sealed what would end up being a 115-111 overtime Game 7 win in Brooklyn to advance to the Eastern Conference Finals for the second time in three seasons.

"As it ended up short, man, just I think we did a good job of tiring him out," Holiday said. "He had a hell of a game. One of the best scorers and players in this league, but to play for that many minutes (53) and have Tuck and K-Midd, Giannis just all over him the whole game and Brook protecting the basket. I just think it kind of tired him out on that last shot. I pressured him as much as possible to try not to get a clear shot and it ended up being short."

Once the ball fell short and the whistle sounded with 0.3 seconds remaining, the Bucks took a timeout. Center Brook Lopez raised his hands in the air and let out a loud yell. He made his way to half court, jumped in the air and slammed down his massive feet on top of the Nets' logo to slap the floor. And then he continued to the Bucks bench, where he was mobbed by his teammates. He hugged them and yelled as they celebrated a hard-fought victory in Brooklyn, their first in five road games against the Nets this season.

For Lopez, that final stop meant the team erased a blunder he made at the end of regulation where he forgot that there were only 2.1 seconds left on the shot clock with

Jrue Holiday struggled shooting the ball in Game 7, making just 5-of-23 shots, but came up big down the stretch and added seven rebounds and eight assists.

8.1 seconds remaining. By failing to take a shot, the Bucks came up with an empty possession and gave the Nets a chance to tie or win the game, which Durant managed to do by forcing overtime. Despite the mistake, Lopez remained determined to pull out a victory.

"After that happened, I just took it upon myself," Lopez said. "I told my teammates, 'I made a mistake, but let's go get this.' I'm gonna fix this, we're gonna fix this and so it happened, but it was great to see how resilient we were."

Lopez's persistence served as a prime example of the resilience of each of the Bucks' five starters, who found a way to contribute to a winning effort on a night where things consistently went wrong with their season on the line.

Despite his mistake at the end of regulation, Lopez came back by contributing a massive block with a minute left in overtime to set up the Bucks' win.

Typically, Lopez waits for offensive players at the rim in the Bucks' drop coverage, but not on this block of Durant. Somehow, Lopez recovered to block Durant's layup attempt from the back side of the defense after Durant rejected the screen and sprinted away from him at full speed.

"He gets all the blocks," Tucker said. "Like, I don't know how he does it, but he does (laughs). That block was amazing and the way we played that was amazing. We always talk about different things we want to do, especially with KD, getting downhill. Being up, being back, it's just so much every possession. It changes so much. He just made a great read and got a great block. It was a huge play."

After the block, the Bucks turned to their favorite set, which puts Khris Middleton in a middle pick-and-roll with Giannis Antetokounmpo. They trusted Middleton, despite the fact that the Bucks' second-leading scorer was just 8-of-24 from the field at the time.

"I don't care," Middleton said of how missed shots affect him. "I don't care how many shots I make. As long as I take great shots, that's all I'm worried about."

Shooting woes or not, Middleton played all 53 minutes of the game, contributing 23 points, 10 rebounds, six assists and five steals. And with the game tied at 111-111 after Lopez's block, Middleton took his time, manipulated the defense and got a great shot to go down to give the Bucks a two-point lead.

Middleton wasn't the only Bucks player to miss a plethora of shots early in the game only to make a clutch bucket late in the game. Before the season, the Bucks traded for Jrue Holiday to replace Eric Bledsoe and serve as the missing piece to get them over the hump in the postseason. When teams gave all their attention to Antetokounmpo and Middleton, he would be able to take over games. After making a stepback jumper with 3:51 remaining in the first quarter, Holiday missed his next 11 shots to bring him to 2-of-17 on the night with the Bucks down 95-91 and 5:39 remaining in regulation. Milwaukee took a timeout.

On the first possession out of that timeout, Holiday ended his personal drought and nailed a catch-and-shoot 3 on an assist from Middleton. Two minutes later, Holiday assisted Antetokounmpo in the pick-and-roll and then scored on three consecutive possessions for the Bucks as they opened up a 107-105 lead with 1:07 remaining in regulation.

"I've been in this league long enough to know that sometimes you're gonna hit 'em and sometimes, you're not," Holiday said. "Sometimes the game is not gonna go your way, but you can't

The Bucks and Nets put together a slugfest of a series, culminating in a memorable Game 7 overtime win for Milwaukee.

be timid, especially in a Game 7, where I'm given the opportunity to come out here and knock these shots down and take these shots."

After Holiday's run gave the Bucks a lead near the end of regulation, Tucker sat in isolation trying to slow down Durant and managed to strip the superstar as he rose up for a jumper. He then continued to harass Durant as Middleton came through with a clutch steal.

"I think there's a toughness with him that's infectious," Budenholzer said. "I think our group was tough before Tuck got here, but he just takes it to that next level."

While the rest of the Bucks' starters seemed to see their redemptive arcs play out while they were on the court, Tucker was forced to watch on the bench and wait for that final Durant miss, which occurred at least partially because of Tucker's dogged determination on the defensive end against Durant for 38 minutes before he fouled out early in the overtime period.

And while the resilience of all the starters stood out in the Bucks' Game 7 win, no one's was more impressive than that of the Bucks' two-time MVP, Giannis Antetokounmpo, who put up 40 points, 13 rebounds and five assists.

From the start of the series, Antetokounmpo listened as people wondered if the moment would be too big for him and the Bucks would fall short in the postseason once again. If he should be taking more shots and scoring more against a lowly-rated Nets defense. Whether he should actually be the one defending Durant.

He had to deal with the slings and arrows that came with his team dropping the first two games of the series in Brooklyn. He had to listen to critics wonder if he should be shooting jumpers or if the Bucks should actually give him the ball in clutch time after he missed a fadeaway jumper over James Harden in the Bucks' Game 5 loss.

It was only fitting that it was Antetokounmpo who put together the strongest performance in the second half of Game 7 and carried the Bucks to a victory.

After watching the Nets limit Antetokounmpo by keeping Blake Griffin away from the pick-and-rolls they ran for Durant and Harden, Budenholzer decided to force Antetokounmpo into the middle of everything the Nets were doing offensively by putting his two-time MVP on Bruce Brown.

"We realized that I was always away from the ball on the reds, the switches," Antetokounmpo said. "So I think great adjustment by coach out of halftime. He told me to switch the matchup, so I can be the guy that switches on KD, James and whoever has the ball."

With Antetokounmpo on Brown, the Bucks messed with the Nets' rhythm to start the half and rattled off a 7-0 run to take a lead in the first two minutes after halftime. From there, the Nets had to work harder on offense with the prospect of Antetokounmpo switching onto Durant or Harden when Brown was used as a screener.

On the other end, Antetokounmpo was in attack mode on his way to 25 points in the second half and overtime, including 16 points in the third quarter. The Bucks' star always insists on trying to make the right play on offense, but admitted early in the series that even when he beats teams with a pass, they don't actually adjust their coverage. They still build the wall like they always do in an effort to keep Antetokounmpo away from the rim.

"That's the amazing thing, he still gets through the walls and still figures his way," Tucker said. "Even making shots, people are going to be there, they're gonna make a choice to make other people beat them, but he still picks and chooses his spots."

Despite a strong start to the second half, the Nets eventually slowed Antetokounmpo down in the final minutes of the game and the first three minutes of overtime. For the first three and a half minutes of overtime, the Bucks went scoreless.

Then, the Bucks made things simple. They gave Antetokounmpo the ball on the block and asked him to score against Durant. Rather than attempting a fadeaway jumper like he did in Game 5 against Harden, Antetokounmpo used his strength

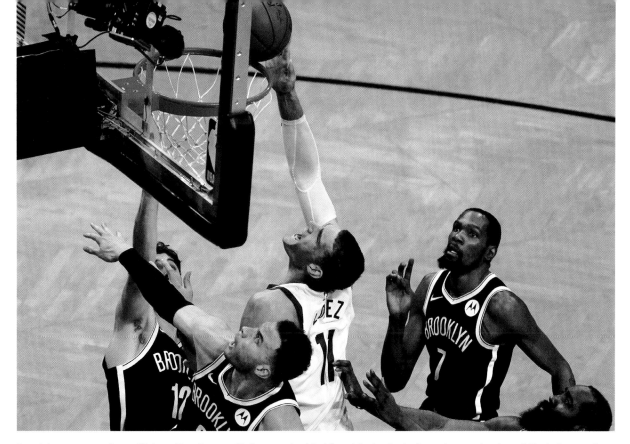

Brook Lopez scored an efficient 19 points on 11 shots and added four blocks, including a huge rejection of Kevin Durant in overtime with a minute remaining.

to back down Durant and get to his hook shot.

When his team needed him most, Antetokounmpo came through in the clutch with a tough bucket and helped the Bucks find a way past the Nets. As the buzzer sounded, Antetokounmpo found himself reflecting on the team's journey in the series.

"I try not to get too high, not to get too low, but I almost got emotional a little bit out there because the team really really tried their best and we kept our composure," Antetokounmpo said. "We were down 2-0. A lot of people didn't believe that we could win back home and we protected our home with our unbelievable fans. Just being able to come to New York and we've already come here five times and we lost five games. We were 0-5. So, just coming to New York again, Game 7 and everybody's anxious. Everybody's nervous and being able to execute, believing one another, trust one another, it was big time."

As has always been the case though, Antetokounmpo wanted his team to keep their

eyes on the bigger prize. The Bucks do not just want to win a second-round series. They want to win a championship, which is why their locker room, whether on the road or at home, features a box in one of the upper corners of the marker board showing how many wins the team has left to win a championship. On Saturday night, it was perhaps fitting that Lopez, after his blunder at the end of regulation and big overtime block (one of the four he came up with Saturday night), did the honors and drew the number "8" on the left corner of the marker board of the visiting locker room at Barclays Center in Brooklyn.

"I'm really happy for this team," Antetokounmpo said. "I'm really happy for what we got done. Really happy that we were able to write '8' on the board, but the job is not done. We got to keep believing ourselves. We got to keep playing good basketball. And take it game-by-game. The job is not done. We're halfway, halfway through." ▰▰▰

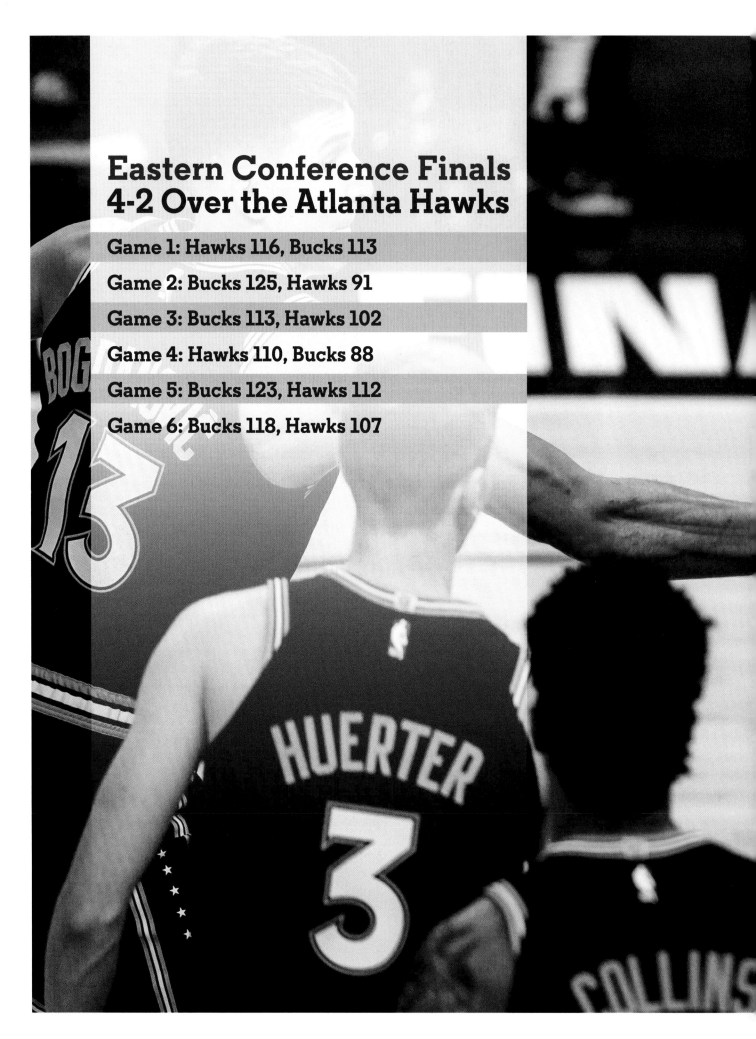

Eastern Conference Finals 4-2 Over the Atlanta Hawks

Game 1: Hawks 116, Bucks 113

Game 2: Bucks 125, Hawks 91

Game 3: Bucks 113, Hawks 102

Game 4: Hawks 110, Bucks 88

Game 5: Bucks 123, Hawks 112

Game 6: Bucks 118, Hawks 107

Apply Pressure

Thanks to Brook Lopez and Jrue Holiday, the Bucks Made Life Tough for Trae Young in Game 2

By Eric Nehm | June 26, 2021

When Hawks guard Trae Young turned the corner on a high pick-and-roll in the first half of Game 1, he knew exactly what he was going to see in front of him. There was going to be a lot of open space and center Brook Lopez waiting for him at the rim. With the Bucks determined to keep Young from getting to the rim and take away his passing lanes to teammates, the Bucks played a rudimentary drop coverage that Young picked apart on his way to 25 points in the first half on 11-of-16 shooting in the Hawks' 116-113 Game 1 win.

Young's view in that same situation was much different during the first half of Game 2.

In Game 2, Lopez stopped waiting for Young at the rim. Instead, the Bucks' 7-foot, 280-pound center stepped up above the free-throw line and attempted to give Young a different look on every possession. Sometimes, his hands were high. Other times, they were low. Often, both of his arms were fully extended to the side of his body and swinging up and down manically like a seesaw controlled by two hyperactive children. Lopez would occasionally fake an extra step toward Young as though he was preparing to crowd his space, only to drop back toward the rim immediately afterward.

"It's all about activity, and that's definitely a point in the game where I can try to have impact, be someone who can make a difference in the game," Lopez (16 points, three steals) said. "I definitely enjoy that."

Lopez kept Young guessing, and it worked as the Bucks' pulled out a 125-91 Game 2 victory. Young put up just 15 points on 6-of-16 shooting and committed a career-high nine turnovers. The Bucks' big man juked and stunted and waved his arms to slow down Young and make him think through a different read on each possession. When asked for a technical term to describe what Lopez was doing on the floor in Game 2, Bucks coach Mike Budenholzer shook his head.

"We just call it Brook," Budenholzer said. "I think I try and stay out of his way, just turn him loose, let him be himself, and that's when he's at his best."

After dropping Game 1 at home, Brook Lopez and the Bucks crushed the Hawks and evened the series in Game 2 with a 125-91 win.

The officials may have missed a kicked ball violation on Jrue Holiday on this first-quarter possession, but just watch Lopez's activity, especially his hands and arms, as Young turned the corner:

Two-time All-Star Khris Middleton has been teammates with Lopez for the entirety of the big man's defensive renaissance over the last three years in Milwaukee, but he knew exactly what Young was going through each time he tried to get downhill on a pick-and-roll. Middleton struggled at the hands of Lopez's juking and stunting cat-and-mouse pick-and-roll defense many times before on the practice floor.

"I hate it," Middleton said with a smile after putting up 15 points, seven rebounds and eight assists in the win. "People don't realize how massive that guy is. I mean, he's a 7-footer, but you feel him around when he's around the rim on the court, even when he's on the perimeter sometimes. I don't think people realize how big he is, how athletic he is, how much ground he can cover, and he's athletic. So that's why I love it when he's on our side during games and not in practice and whatnot."

While the Bucks' defensive excellence Friday night had much to do with Lopez's unique brilliance, one of the game's first possessions put the team's collective aptitude on display, neutralizing a pick-and-roll at the moment Young picked up his dribble.

Lopez picked up Young out past the right elbow, but his increased pressure did not force Young into holding the ball a step inside the 3-point line; that was Middleton.

Rather than remain connected to the Hawks' shooters as they did in Game 1, Middleton abandoned Solomon Hill in the right corner to interrupt Young. With his dribble terminated, Young's options became more limited and the Bucks could play even more aggressively. Giannis Antetokounmpo, like Middleton, slid into a strong help position, and that took away the initial bounce pass to Clint Capela and forced Young to

keep his drive going and ultimately jump in the air to create a different angle, which Lopez took away to force a turnover.

"It just crowds the whole space for everybody, and we have to do our job," Antetokounmpo (25 points, nine rebounds and six assists) said. "So it's the least we can do, but I think that really makes a big difference like showing, being in driving lanes, showing help and making other guys make the play so (Young) can pass the ball."

The Bucks were still in drop coverage in Game 2, but as they had done in their first two series against the Heat and Nets, the Bucks' coaching staff tweaked their base drop coverage from the regular season and molded it into a unique form suited for slowing down the Hawks. It confused Young to such an extent that the game was over by the time both teams made their way to their respective locker rooms. Young recorded eight first-half turnovers, four of which occurred in the middle of a Bucks' 20-0 second-quarter run that ballooned Milwaukee's halftime lead to 77-45.

After watching the film from Game 2, Young will likely find some adjustments to take advantage of the Bucks' newly modified drop coverage and make himself a more dangerous playmaker. He may be able to make the Bucks pay for leaving the strong-side corner or the weak-side wing and create open 3-pointers for some of the Hawks shooters. And he may realize he can manipulate the helpers that tried to cut off the driving lanes for him in Game 2 by keeping his dribble alive more often, but even then, Holiday will still be his primary defender, and that will continue to make things difficult.

After the game, Holiday explained that he believed he was "smarter" defending Young for a second straight game, despite doing many of the same things he did in Game 1.

"I think just mix it up, make it difficult for him, not get too many easy looks," Holiday said following a 22-point, seven-assist performance. "Last game, he was living in the paint, had a lot of

Jrue Holiday added 22 points and seven assists in the comfortable win, and locked up Trae Young, who was limited to only 15 points on 6-of-16 shooting.

floaters, was pretty much there for him. We didn't really want to get him started early, and I don't think he went to the free-throw line much tonight, which is also pretty big for us."

Holiday got physical with Young in Game 2 and managed to end the game with just two personal fouls, which meant he managed to impose his will with Young without putting himself in a compromised position. The Bucks' First Team All-Defense guard did a better job finishing plays Friday as well. Rather than watch Young get past him and then go for a late rear contest on a floater or trail the play entirely, Holiday kept himself in a position to make things more difficult on Young.

On top of working his way back into passing lanes for steals, Holiday also figured out a way to make Young uncomfortable while shooting pull-up 3-pointers, and it had nothing to do with being physical or crowding Young. In fact, it was the exact opposite. When the Hawks star decided to

shoot a pull-up 3 against Holiday, the Bucks point guard opted against boxing out and just sprinted down the court for a few easy layups.

It may not actually affect Young's shot, but there could also be a small part of him that now knows every time he tries a 3-pointer and holds his follow-through, Holiday will be at the opposite 3-point line by the time the Bucks collect the rebound.

Holiday's leakouts were just another smart tweak in the Bucks' game plan to make Young more uncomfortable Friday. They did not make wholesale changes to their defense to do it either. Instead of taking Lopez off the floor in favor of switchy, small-ball units, the Bucks leaned on their big man and surrounded him with more aggressive help defenders. With Holiday putting pressure on the ball and better help around him, the Bucks fully unleashed Lopez and left Young wondering what happened to the easy looks he got in Game 1. ▬▬

'I Trust This Guy to Death'

Giannis Antetokounmpo Sings Khris Middleton's Praises After Game 3 Heroics

By Eric Nehm | June 28, 2021

Giannis Antetokounmpo did not like Khris Middleton during his first NBA season. In fact, he hated Middleton during the 2013-14 campaign.

Just over a month after drafting Antetokounmpo in the summer of 2013, the Bucks traded their starting point guard Brandon Jennings to the Detroit Pistons for Brandon Knight and Middleton, a throw-in to even up the slight difference in the swap of starting point guards. While Antetokounmpo would eventually be a breakout star, it was Middleton who appeared in the starting lineup in the Bucks' season opener, not the 18-year-old Antetokounmpo.

As the skinny rookie from Greece tried to fight for more playing time under then-head coach Larry Drew, Antetokounmpo scratched and clawed for minutes in the rotation against Middleton, literally. As Antetokounmpo recounted to The Athletic two years ago, he used to go home after practices and show his parents the scratches on his arms that came from hand-fighting with Middleton to keep the 22-year-old wing from getting open shots in practice.

On Sunday night, when reminded of those fights after watching Middleton, his teammate of eight seasons, rain down clutch bucket possession after possession and score 20 of his 38 points in the fourth quarter to lead the Bucks to a 113-102 Game 3 victory, Antetokounmpo smiled thinking back to the playing time battles in their first season together in Milwaukee.

"It's an unbelievable journey," Antetokounmpo said after putting up 33 points and 11 rebounds in the win.

The brief trip down memory lane made Antetokounmpo wistful and it inspired him to tell reporters just how much Middleton means to him now, eight years after they were first introduced to one another.

Khris Middleton and Giannis Antetokounmpo have been through plenty of ups and downs as teammates for the Bucks since 2013 and have emerged from it as an incredible duo with complimentary skills.

"It's crazy we were talking about maybe like, I don't know, maybe like a few days ago, four days ago, five days in the locker room and we were talking about like, "How long are you going to play for?" Antetokounmpo recounted. "We just had a silly conversation. And he was like — I'm not going to say exactly what he said, but I told him, 'Hey, the day you retire is going to be the toughest day in my career because like I've been with you the whole time.'

"And it's been an unbelievable journey. It's great seeing this guy, man, the way we started, the way we are, the way he started and the way that he is right now, just closing games. That's what we need from Khris. We need him to be aggressive. We need him to be taking over games, make good decisions, and play off him."

Before Sunday's Game 3, according to Basketball-Reference, Antetokounmpo and Middleton had shared the floor for 573 games — 517 in the regular season and 56 in the playoffs — as members of the Milwaukee Bucks. And yet, despite that extensive shared history, Antetokounmpo still found himself trying to figure out what exactly Middleton was doing in the middle of the fourth quarter as the game hung in the balance.

"It was strange to me," Antetokounmpo said.

With the Bucks trailing 95-88 and 7:32 remaining in Game 3, Middleton nailed a 3-pointer when Hawks forward John Collins gave him too much space on the right wing. After Pat Connaughton scored a fast-break bucket off of a P.J. Tucker steal, the Bucks got another stop and Middleton hit another right-wing 3 to give the Bucks a 96-95 lead on an 8-0 run. Young immediately answered with a 3-pointer of his own to regain the lead and that is when Middleton confused his long-time running mate.

"Jrue was on the right side of the floor and I was in the middle," Antetokounmpo said of the Bucks' spacing as they brought the ball up the floor. "And (Middleton) was like in the (far) left corner, right? He was begging for the ball. And I'm looking and

I'm like, 'He's not open.'"

"But like Jrue took the ball, swing it to Pat or somebody, and then he swing it to Khris and Khris like pump-faked, try to drive the ball, did not drive the ball, came to the three-point line, took a step to the corner like almost like behind-the-backboard, cash. That's greatness to me."

While the lead-up to the shot was unusual to Antetokounmpo, the shot itself looked quite familiar.

After the Bucks took Game 2 against the Hawks in Milwaukee, Middleton claimed Antetokounmpo's spectacular right-handed, double-pump finger roll was something he had never seen his teammate do before, not even in their one-on-one sessions on the practice court. Antetokounmpo, however, could not say the same about Middleton's step-back fadeaway jumper to tie the game at 98.

"He's done that when we play one-on-one a lot of times," Antetokounmpo said. "And I think one thing that over time that he got better at, especially against me, is that he learned how to like use his body and his shoulders and his stops to like shoot over me. He's really elite in that."

With no playing time on the line, that type of thing no longer upsets Antetokounmpo, right? His defense on Middleton in practice settings can only help his teammate improve in future games. So, as Antetokounmpo and Middleton star together on one of the league's best teams and sit just two wins away from the NBA Finals, there is no way Antetokounmpo still gets angry about his Bucks brother besting him in a one-on-one bout, right?

Wrong.

"Mad as hell," Antetokounmpo said of how he feels when Middleton hits a tough shot over him in practice. "Because he's one of those players that you play great defense and you're right there, and you're like, 'Okay, I got him. I got him. He can't go nowhere.' And all of a sudden, he's just — rainbow shot over the top of you, cash. But he's special for a reason, and he showed it tonight."

Middleton was spectacular in Game 3,

contributing 38 points, 12 rebounds and seven assists. He hit eight of the 13 shots he attempted in the fourth quarter and carried the Bucks to a road victory.

While most fans would not put Middleton at the top of their list of the NBA's most clutch performers, Sunday was just another installment in a series of big-time playoff performances from Middleton this postseason. When the Bucks needed a bucket late in Game 1 of their first-round series against the Heat, they put the ball in Middleton's hands and he delivered with the game-winning jumper. In a win-or-stay-home Game 6 in the Nets series, Middleton scored a playoff-career-high 38 points (a number he tied Sunday against the Hawks) and then followed that up by hitting what ended up being the game-winning bucket in overtime of the Bucks' Game 7 win over the Nets.

As the Bucks have grown with Mike Budenholzer at the helm over the last three seasons, Middleton has turned into the team's closer. When the Bucks need a score late in games, they give the ball to Middleton and let him make a play, so no one in the Bucks' locker room was surprised to see him come up big when the team needed to make a comeback late in Game 3.

"He's a winner," Bucks coach Mike Budenholzer said. "From the (first) day I've been around him, he's done nothing but win. He does all the little things. He's quiet but his voice is loud in our locker room. His voice is loud in our time-outs. So I think he's just one of those guys that's very smooth and just has a way of playing and can score in ways that I think kind of sneak up on people."

Many teams around the league would not trust end-of-game situations to a former second-round pick like Middleton. He is not explosive off-the-dribble or overwhelmingly strong to create shots at the rim. There are not many easy buckets in his offensive repertoire, but the Bucks have never wavered in their trust of Middleton in the biggest moments and much of that has to do with Antetokounmpo. Despite winning back-to-back MVPs, the Bucks' superstar does not care whether or not he takes the big shots for the Bucks.

"I trust this guy to death," Antetokounmpo said. "If he wants the ball, he gets it. Simple as that. He was knocking down shots. Doesn't really matter who is the first guy, second — it does not matter. We play basketball and we try to win games.

"I want to be a winner. I have the whole game to be 'the guy.' I don't care about being the guy in the fourth quarter. Whoever wants to be the guy in the fourth quarter, Khris or Jrue or P.J. or Bobby or Bryn or whoever the case might be and help us win games, that's what I care about. But yeah, I trust Khris to death. If Khris asks for the ball, better give him the ball."

On Sunday, the Bucks gave Middleton the ball repeatedly throughout the fourth quarter and watched as he outscored the Hawks, 20-17, by himself. For some superstars, it might have been tough to put their ego aside and watch as their teammate took over the game, but not Antetokounmpo. He knows he needs his teammates to play well to take the next step in his career and reach the NBA Finals, so Antetokounmpo was more than happy to step aside and just watch the show.

"Greatness. What I saw today was unbelievable. He was freaking unbelievable, carried the team at the end," Antetokounmpo said. "We were like, get the hell out of the way, give him the ball, take us home, Khris, and that's what he did. I talked to him a little bit in the locker room, and what I saw today was unbelievable and for me, it was greatness, simple as that."

That greatness has Antetokounmpo and Middleton, the practice court combatants, just two wins away from standing side-by-side in the starting lineup for the Bucks' first NBA Finals appearance since 1974.

Not too bad for two dudes who hated each other eight years ago, huh? ▬▬

Rise Together

How the Bucks Replaced Giannis Antetokounmpo's Production to Knock on the Door of the NBA Finals

By Eric Nehm | July 2, 2021

As Jrue Holiday snaked his drive through the lane from right to left, he saw one of the Hawks' help defenders put themselves out of position. So he did what he has always done as a member of the Bucks. He threw a lob high and into the open area.

Unfortunately, his alley-oop was off-target, but it didn't matter. His big man managed to catch it and slam it home anyways. "He dunked it so hard," Bobby Portis said. "That was crazy. I didn't think he had a chance of even catching that."

"That joint was crazy," Holiday said. "Like he made me look good because I threw a bad pass."

Typically, that would be the kind of thing said about an alley-oop to Giannis Antetokounmpo, but with the Bucks' star out of the lineup for Game 5 with a hyperextended left knee, it was actually Brook Lopez on the receiving end of his bad pass. And miraculously, Lopez threw down the one-handed dunk with authority.

"Hey man, Brook's the MVP," Holiday said.

While Holiday was having a little fun with the idea of the 7-foot, 280-pound Lopez looking like the insanely athletic Greek Freak, Lopez actually did his best Antetokounmpo impression by dominating in the paint in the Bucks' 123-112 Game 5 victory and scoring a career playoff-high 33 points on 14-of-18 shooting with the two-time NBA MVP sidelined because of a hyperextended left knee.

Lopez was far from alone in putting up big numbers in the win. In fact, he wasn't even alone in putting up a playoff career-high as Bobby Portis did the same thing with 22 points. Holiday played spectacularly and led the Bucks with 13 assists to go along with 25 points, while Khris Middleton was solid with 26 points, 13 rebounds and six assists in 45 minutes.

With Giannis out of the lineup, the Bucks knew they had a monumental task in front of them. Not only did they need to figure out how to replace roughly 30 points, 10 rebounds and six assists, they also needed to do that while playing winning basketball and grabbing Game 5 of the 2021 Eastern Conference finals.

After a Game 4 loss to the Hawks, the series was even and the Bucks were in a precarious spot with Giannis Antetokounmpo's knee injury and uncertain status. Brook Lopez and his teammates responded to the adversity in a Game 5 win, with Lopez putting together a dominant performance of 33 points, seven rebounds and four blocks.

"Obviously, no one can replace Giannis," Lopez said. "He's a freaking two-time MVP and so much of what we do. No one person is going to replace that. It's a matter of everyone stepping up and I think everyone showed that they're capable of doing that tonight."

While the Bucks' center scored more points than anyone else in Game 5, the team's collective effort to make up for the absence of their two-time MVP started with their point guard. After a Game 4 effort that multiple players described as disappointing following the game, the Bucks wanted to make sure they were the more aggressive team in Game 5 and Holiday made that clear on the Bucks' first offensive possession.

"I like playing that way," Holiday said. "I'm a bigger guard, so I could take that. I like being physical. I like getting into the paint. Especially when Giannis, our main guy, is getting to the paint especially in transition, he has the advantage of a mismatch. I just felt like I had to do my part today."

Holiday scored seven of the Bucks' first 10 points and attacked the rim relentlessly in the first quarter as the Bucks took a 30-10 lead to start the game. Once Holiday showed off his scoring prowess, he made sure to get the rest of his teammates involved, starting with the man in the middle. As Holiday broke down the defense, Lopez sprinted to the front of the rim and tried to find the perfect pocket of space for a pass from Holiday — a role typically reserved for Antetokounmpo, but filled admirably by Lopez in Game 5.

Typically, Antetokounmpo is the player who flashes into the open space in front of the rim on drives. He is normally the man who gets the first crack at finding the space for a pocket pass or the vertical spacing for an alley-oop, while Lopez stands behind the 3-point line attempting to create open spaces for Antetokounmpo. With Antetokounmpo out of the picture and Portis

playing Lopez's typical role, the lane was wide-open for Lopez to take Antetokounmpo's spot at the rim. Rather than stand out behind the 3-point line, Lopez cut down the lane with authority and made himself available to Holiday, something he has rarely gotten the chance to do since joining the Bucks as a stretch five.

"It was definitely fun," Lopez said. "Giannis gets to do that. I'm usually watching him. But it's easy when you have guys like Jrue and Khris who are making plays like that. They draw so much attention, command so much attention and rightfully so. They know how to make that extra pass, that play to whoever it is, if it's me diving or Bobby or Pat in the corner, P.J. in the corner, whatever it is, they know how to make that play."

To that end, Holiday assisted on seven of Lopez's 14 baskets on the night. Holiday's ability to beat defenders off the dribble and then find Lopez fueled the Bucks' offensive attack.

"I think me and Brook kind of have this connection, defensively and offensively, just for him to be able to get in positions to help me," Holiday said. "So even when I get into the paint, and sometimes his man might step up, I always know that Brook's right behind him."

As the Hawks tried to figure out how to slow down the Holiday-Lopez connection in the first half, they also needed to contend with Portis. The six-year NBA forward made his first postseason start in place of Antetokounmpo and did not waste the opportunity. The Fiserv Forum fan-favorite flew around the floor on both sides of the ball. He tied a career playoff-high in points, but also steals (with three) and perfectly played his role on defense as the Bucks decided to switch all five players in pick-and-roll actions in Game 5. And with the Bucks' defense getting stops in the first half, Portis sprinted down the floor for easy buckets, something he has prided himself on doing all season long in Milwaukee.

"He brings this energy that nobody else could bring," Holiday said. "It doesn't matter how he's playing, but he's going to muck it up, he's going to fight, he's going to talk, and everybody loves when somebody talks. He knows that we got his back. So, love the way that he plays and continues to play. He's been huge for us."

With Holiday, Lopez and Portis in control of the game in the first three quarters, Middleton chipped in when needed, but did not force anything. When Holiday took his final break of the game with the Bucks leading, 91-78, to start the fourth quarter, Budenholzer put the ball in Middleton's hands on the first five possessions of the fourth quarter to close out the game. Here is a summary of what happened on those possessions:

- Pick-and-roll with Lopez — made Middleton 20-foot jumper
- Pick-and-roll with Lopez — Middleton assist for Forbes 3
- Pick-and-roll with Lopez — made Middleton pull-up 3 from the top of the key
- Right wing iso drive — Middleton assist to Lopez for hook shot in the lane
- Pick-and-roll with Lopez — missed wide-open Tucker corner 3 on a potential assist from Middleton

The assist to Forbes, in particular, showcased Middleton's mastery of pick-and-roll basketball.

"With Giannis out, Donte (DiVincenzo) out, we don't have as many ballhandlers," Middleton said. "I think it was myself and Bryn as guards out there, and I think we'd rather have Bryn off the ball to be ready to shoot more. Put the ball in my hands and read pick-and-roll. And after that, just play the game, read the defense. Read where my shots are coming from and read where I get the ball to Brook or other guys. It's just playing within a flow and reading a defense out of a pick-and-roll."

The Hawks hit seven of the 15 3-pointers they attempted in the fourth quarter to keep the game somewhat close until the very end, but the Bucks had an answer. Whether it was Holiday or Middleton or Lopez or Portis, the Bucks handled the Hawks' pressure in the final period and closed out the win to put the Bucks just one win away from the NBA Finals. All four players scored 20 points and took over the game during different portions of the game to grab a pivotal Game 5 victory without their best player.

"I just think with Giannis being out, people had to step up," Holiday said. "People knew that they were going to get shots and opportunities, and to step into those with confidence and make those. Everybody who had 20 today is capable of doing that every single game, but we also know our roles. I think for them to be able to do that and step up in a game like this is huge. It's a fun way to play, with everybody sharing and scoring and everybody is contributing, so we want to continue doing that."

Antetokounmpo's timeline to return to the floor is unclear. The Bucks have given no indication if he will be ready to play in Game 6 or a potential Game 7. Nor is it clear if he would even be able to play in the NBA Finals, if the Bucks manage to advance. But for one night, that did not matter. For one night, the rest of the Bucks' roster showed off its skills and picked up a major postseason victory without Antetokounmpo on the floor. ▬▬▬

Questions? Answered.

The Bucks Are Going to the NBA Finals

By Eric Nehm | July 4, 2021

For the last three seasons, multiple variations of a single question lingered around the Milwaukee Bucks.

Are the Bucks around Giannis Antetokounmpo good enough?

The question manifested itself in many forms, but no matter what role someone played in the organization, the question remained. And the question mutated and multiplied until it ultimately grew into its most exaggerated shape in the days and weeks leading up to the moment Giannis Antetokounmpo became eligible to sign his supermax extension last offseason. As days passed and Antetokounmpo still had not signed the extension, the questions grew louder.

Is Khris Middleton good enough to be the No. 2 option on a title contender? Is Jrue Holiday good enough to convince Antetokounmpo the Bucks are serious about winning? Is the rest of the roster good enough to give the Bucks' stars the support they need in a title run? Is Mike Budenholzer good enough to make the adjustments needed to put the Bucks over the top? Is Jon Horst good enough to pick out the savvy moves needed to put together a championship roster?

With a 118-107 victory in Game 6 of the Eastern Conference Finals to send the Bucks to their first NBA Finals since 1974, the Bucks authored a definitive response to those questions:

Enough.

With a chance to close out the Hawks in Game 6 on the road with Antetokounmpo sidelined for a second straight game because of a hyperextended left knee, Middleton, the player some doubted could consistently be a 20-point-per-game scorer, scored 23 points in the third quarter alone on his way to 32 points, four rebounds and seven assists. It was the second time in the series Middleton had scored at least 20 points in a quarter (fourth quarter of Game 3) on the road.

Jrue Holiday and the Bucks closed out the Hawks in Game 6, with Holiday stuffing the box score with 27 points, nine rebounds, nine assists, four steals and two blocks, while also helping hold a hobbled Trae Young to 14 points on 4-of-17 shooting.

After a putrid first half that included six turnovers, Middleton took control of the game in the second half by scoring the Bucks' first 16 points of the third quarter. just three and a half minutes into the second half, Middleton's outburst ultimately became an individual 16-2 run where he opened up a 63-47 lead for the Bucks after they led by just four at halftime.

"He's the type of player that he puts all the weight on his shoulders and doesn't care," Holiday said (27 points, nine rebounds and nine assists) after the win. "He's like, 'Come on.'"

And throughout that entire run, Middleton just did what he always has done. He used his dribble, length and craftiness to create shots for himself that he buried, even with defenders putting a hand in his face.

"I feel like everything that happened last year and the previous years, people always talking about how they didn't have enough or how they didn't do this or do that; I feel like Khris, man, he's been that person," Holiday said. "He's been that guy."

After Middleton's hot shooting petered out in the fourth quarter, the Hawks trimmed the Bucks lead to just six points, 107-101, with 3:41 remaining. In an ideal world, Middleton's hot-shooting night would have paired with a huge performance by Antetokounmpo, but with no Greek Freak on the floor and the Hawks defense tilted in Middleton's direction, the Bucks needed somebody else to step up. And that was the moment Holiday stepped up, put his head down to get to the rim and made one of the most ridiculous lay-ups of the entire season.

In doing so, Holiday showed exactly why the Bucks gave up three first-round picks and two more potential first-round pick swaps to get him in Milwaukee.

"I think pressure is often external, right," Pat Connaughton (13 points, eight rebounds) said. "So internally within the team, we just love playing with him. We love having him on board. We love the type of guy he is as a person. As a player, he always makes the right play. When he's in attack mode he's really hard to stop not just from a scoring standpoint but from getting other guys involved, getting guys easy shots, getting open shots, whatever it might be."

With Antetokounmpo out for the final two games of the series, Holiday stepped up in a major way alongside Middleton. After a disappointing Game 4 loss that evened the series, the Bucks re-focused their effort and took two straight games from the Hawks with both Holiday and Middleton playing a major role. In Games 5 and 6, Holiday averaged 26 points, 7.5 rebounds and 11 assists per game, while Middleton put up 29 points per game, 8.5 rebounds and 7.5 assists.

But they were not alone. They got help from up and down the Bucks' roster to close out the series.

The Bucks could not have won the final two games against the Hawks without their triumvirate of big men that started alongside Middleton and Holiday. Brook Lopez stepped up in a major way offensively with 33 points in Game 5, but his ability to execute a switching defense in both games allowed the Bucks to stifle everything the Hawks wanted to do across both games. Bobby Portis and P.J. Tucker hit the offensive glass with as much force as possible and kept multiple possessions alive across the final two games of the series. The Bucks bench of Pat Connaughton, Bryn Forbes, Jeff Teague and Thanasis Antetokounmpo scored 29 points in the Game 6 win.

"As a head coach, I feel fortunate to have been

Behind Khris Middleton's 32 points and seven assists, the Bucks clinched their first NBA Finals berth since 1974.

through this experience and kind of have seen it from a different seat (as an assistant coach), but now to do it as a head coach is special," Budenholzer said of making his first Finals appearance as a head coach. "But it's the players that do it. I love our group. I love coaching them. I'm happy for them. When I take a second tonight, when we take a second tonight, it's really just joy and happiness for your players; that they put the work in, the time to get to this place, and just be happy for them."

While Budenholzer gave the credit to the players on the roster assembled by general manager Jon Horst, the Bucks might not have made it to the Finals without Budenholzer leaving his comfort zone and trying new things. The series was tied at two when Budenholzer changed the Bucks' defensive scheme and asked his big men to get slightly uncomfortable and switch one through five in ball screens, which meant covering smaller guards that would try to drive by them. And while he may not describe it as uncomfortable, that change meant Budenholzer moved away from the drop pick-and-roll coverage that had led to the Bucks putting together the league's best regular season defense the last two seasons.

"He's done more adjusting this year than he's ever done before, schemes and some of the things that we're doing, he's getting a little more adventurous," Tucker said. "And I think the personnel, that gives him a freedom to do that a lot more and that's one of the reasons we've been so successful."

By embracing change and trying new defensive strategies, Budenholzer and the Bucks pulled out a hard-fought series against the Hawks in the Eastern Conference finals and celebrated the franchise's first NBA Finals appearance in 47 years. With their star watching from the sideline for the final two games of the series, Antetokounmpo's teammates answered all the questions that had been asked of them over the previous three seasons.

They are good enough.

And Antetokounmpo made sure to let all of them know that in the series clincher.

"This is probably the most I've seen Giannis talk, like the whole game," Holiday said. "I know usually when he's on the court and he's running, racing through five people and blocking shots, I mean, you're tired. He's tired and he's playing. But man, he's motivating everybody, he's motivating me, telling me to push the pace, telling me to keep being aggressive and telling me to lock people up."

After every big play in Game 6, Antetokounmpo was there. After a big offensive rebound, Antetokounmpo yelled or flexed as the situation deemed necessary. As his teammates got back onto the floor after a timeout, Antetokounmpo walked with his teammates or pulled them aside to give them a piece of advice. And when they pulled out the victory, Antetokounmpo celebrated with them.

As the time ticked off the clock and the buzzer sounded on Game 6, Middleton made his way through the line of Hawks walking down the sideline to extend his appreciation for a hard-fought series. Antetokounmpo did the same thing but took a more circuitous route out onto the floor. As both finished up their conversations, they made their way back toward the Bucks bench. A few coaches stopped Middleton around midcourt, while Antetokounmpo slowly weaved through remaining Hawks staffers and eventually met Middleton at halfcourt.

Antetokounmpo yelled at Middleton and they embraced. Around the same time, Bucks coach Mike Budenholzer freed up from the mob of people on the floor and looked on briefly before getting to give Middleton a hug of his own. As he was asked about it after the game, Budenholzer smiled and then choked up briefly before talking about the moment.

With the answers surrounding his supporting cast answered, the attention will turn once again toward Antetokounmpo and his health status. The

Even though Giannis Antetokounmpo couldn't play in Game 6 due to a knee injury, he provided guidance and emotional support for his teammates throughout the game and had plenty of energy left to celebrate the historic win with head coach Mike Budenholzer.

Bucks managed to get through two games of the Eastern Conference Finals without their superstar leading the charge, but to secure a championship, the Bucks will need him back on the floor to beat a Suns squad that is more than good enough as well.

"Khris and Giannis are the key to this team, the key to this organization," Budenholzer said. "To have the opportunity to coach them and come here three years ago and try and build something special, those two guys are special, and it starts with them. Just feel incredibly fortunate to coach those two guys."

Their teammates feel the same way.

"Khris is the heart of this team," Holiday said. "I feel like Giannis is the soul of this team, and without them, man, we really wouldn't be here."

But the special moment ended there. The Bucks have another series to play and four more wins to pick up to win the franchise's first NBA championship since 1971. According to the players, the team's celebration in the visiting locker room in Atlanta was subdued and the reason why was simple.

"We ain't did nothing yet," Tucker said. ▬▬